BASEBALL RULES ILLUSTRATED

BY
LOUIS PHILLIPS AND ARNIE MARKOE

A FIRESIDE BOOK
Published by Simon & Schuster, Inc. New York

Copyright © 1982 by Simon & Schuster, Inc.

All rights reserved
including the right of reproduction
in whole or in part in any form

First Fireside Edition, 1985

Published by Simon & Schuster, Inc.
Simon & Schuster Building
Rockefeller Center
1230 Avenue of the Americas
New York, New York 10020

FIRESIDE and colophon are registered trademarks of
Simon & Schuster, Inc.

Designed by

Manufactured in the United States of America

    3 4 5 6 7 8 9 10

Library of Congress Cataloging-in-Publication Data
Main entry under title:

Baseball rules illustrated.

    "A Fireside book."
    1. Baseball—Rules.   I. Phillips, Louis.
II. Markoe, Arnie.
GV877.B3354   1985   796.357'02'022   85-14557
ISBN 0-671-61136-4

CONTENTS

INTRODUCTION

The best place to begin, as *Alice in Wonderland* reminds us, is at the beginning. The best introduction to a book of this nature is not to be found in any elaborate essay but in the rules of the game itself—the very first set of baseball rules as adopted by the Knickerbocker Baseball Club of New York on September 23, 1845.

Rule 1. Members must strictly observe the time agreed upon for the commencement of the game, and be punctual in their attendance.

Rule 2. Before the commencement of the game the President shall appoint an umpire, who shall keep the game in a book provided for that purpose, and note all violations of the rules during the game.

Rule 3. The two Captains shall toss for innings; the winner having the choice of sending his team first to the bat or to the field.

Rule 4. The bases shall be from "home" to second base, 42 paces; from first to third base, 42 paces equidistant.

Rule 5. No stump (or scrub) game shall be played on the regular day of a match game.

Rule 6. If a sufficient number of members should not be present at the hour named for commencing the game, their places may be filled by gentlemen not regular members of the Club.

Rule 7. If members appear after the game has commenced, they may be chosen in if mutually agreed upon.

Rule 8. The game is to consist of twenty-one counts, or aces, but at the conclusion an equal number of hands may be played.

Rule 9. The ball must be pitched, not thrown to the batter.

Rule 10. A ball knocked out of the field, or outside the range of the first or third base, is foul.

Rule 11. Three balls being struck at and missed and the last one caught, is a hand-out; if not caught it is considered fair, and the striker bound to run.

9

Rule 12. If a ball be struck, or tipped, and caught either flying or on the first bound, it is a handout.

Rule 13. A player running the bases shall be out if the ball is in the hands of an adversary on the base, or the runner is touched with it before he makes his base; it being understood, however, that in no instance is a ball to be thrown at him.

Rule 14. A player running who shall prevent an adversary from catching or getting the ball before making his base, is a handout.

Rule 15. Three handouts, all out.

Rule 16. Players must take their strike in regular turn.

Rule 17. All disputes and differences relative to the game to be decided by the Umpire, from which there is no appeal.

Rule 18. No ace or base can be made on a foul strike.

Rule 19. A runner cannot be put out in making one base, when a balk is made by the Pitcher.

Rule 20. But one base allowed when a ball bounds off the field when struck.

In 1848 the following rule was added:
Rule 21. The player running to first base is out if the ball is held by an adversary on that base before the runner reaches it, but this applies to first base only.

In 1854 the following rules were added:
Rule 22. Players must make the bases in order of striking, and when a fair ball is struck and the striker not put out, the first base must be vacated as well as the next base or bases if similarly occupied; players must be put out under these circumstances, in the same manner as when running to first base.

Rule 23. A player shall be out, if at any time when off a base he shall be touched by the ball in the hands of an adversary.

Rule 24. If two hands are already out, a player running home at the time a ball is struck cannot make an ace if the striker is caught out or put out at first base.

Rule 25. Players must take their strike in regular rotation; and after the first inning is played the turn commences at the player who stands on the list next to the one who lost the third hand.

Rule 26. The ball shall weigh from five and a half to six ounces, and measure from two and three-quarters to three and one-half inches in diameter.

(*Addition to rule 4.* From Home to Pitcher not less than 15 paces.)

In 1857 the following rule was added:
Rule 27. A game shall consist of nine innings and at least five innings must be played to constitute a game.

In December of 1861, the National Association of Baseball Players met and adopted a rule that fixed the weight and measurement of the baseball itself:

The ball must not weigh less than five and one-half, nor more than five and three-fourth ounces avoirdupois. It must measure not less than nine and three-fourth inches in

circumference. It must be composed of India-rubber and yarn, covered with leather, and, in all match games, shall be furnished by the challenging club, and become the property of the winning club, as a trophy of victory.

Three years later, at the convention of 1864, the so-called fair fly rule was adopted, which stipulated that the catch of a fair ball on the first bounce could no longer put a man out. And so on. At one time, batters could use a bat shaved flat on one side; runners could be put out by being hit with the baseball; home plate was a solid-iron disk.

But the character of a game is determined by its rules. Baseball's rules have changed to protect the players, excite the fans, add money to the coffers of the owners, and enhance the quality of the game. Whereas there were only thirty-eight official rules in 1861, there are hundreds of simple and complex rules today. A comparison of the rules of 1845 and 1861 with those of today shows clearly how far baseball has come, evolving from game to sport to business. And yet, somehow, it has remained at its core the same. From its very beginnings to the present, baseball has been America's quintessential sport.

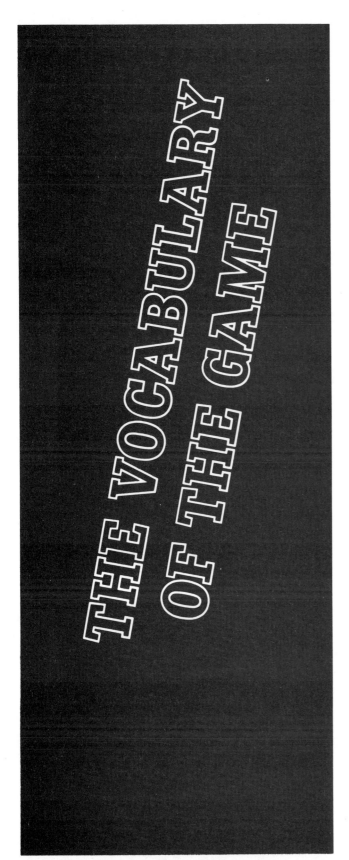

THE VOCABULARY OF THE GAME

Baseball speaks two distinct languages. There is the formal lexicon of the game itself, consisting of terms like bunt, batter's box, foul ball. Then there is the language of the players and fans and sportscasters—the colorful slang expressions you are likely to come across in the stands or in the dugout or in written accounts of the game. Part I of this vocabulary gives the essential terms of baseball, while Part II gives examples of baseball slang.

I. Baseball Terms

appeal   A claim by a fielder to an umpire that there has been a breach of the rules by the offensive team. *Example:* On a call of balls and strikes, the catcher appeals to the third base umpire to determine whether or not the batter has gone far enough around on his swing for a strike.

assist   The credit given by the official scorer to a fielder who has handled the baseball or has even deflected the ball in such a manner that the fielder has helped put out a player.

balk   A motion by the pitcher that entitles all runners on base to advance one base. The three most common types of balks include

1) the pitcher stopping his delivery when he is already committed to making a pitch;
2) the pitcher failing to come to a complete stop when he brings his hands down from the stretch; and
3) the pitcher allowing the ball to slip out of his hand while his foot is on the rubber.

In a major league baseball game, the umpire is allowed considerable discretion in determining if the pitcher has committed an illegal act or balk.

ball   A pitch that is outside the strike zone of the batter and is not swung at by the batter. Four balls allow the batter to take first base (see **base on balls**).

base   Any one of four points on the diamond—first base, second base, third base, and home. In the 1840's, the first bases were wooden posts, but players were often injured by running into them, so stones were substituted. Finally, sacks of sand that were fastened down with chains came into use. Running around the base paths, a runner must touch the bases or be ruled out.

base coach   A uniformed member of the offensive team who stands in a designated area behind first or third base (the coach's box) and signals instructions to the batter and runners. In general, a coach directs traffic and advises runners whether to stay on a given base or to run.

base hit   A baseball struck by the batter in such a manner that the fielders cannot reach it in time to throw the batter out. Usually called a hit.

base on balls   A walk. The award of first base to a batter who has received four pitches outside the strike zone.

batter   The offensive player who takes his turn at bat by stepping into the batter's box and who receives pitches thrown at him by the pitcher. In an official game, the batter must bat in the order assigned to him by his manager.

batter's box   A space defined by chalked lines in which the batter must stand while swinging at a pitched ball (see diagram on page 36, Layout at Home Base).

battery   The pitcher and the catcher. In war, a battery is two or more pieces of artillery constituting a tactical unit. Since the pitcher and the catcher supply the firepower to the game, they came to be called the battery.

bench   Place where team members and coaches sit when they are not on the field. A player who is kept out of the game, perhaps because of injuries or poor play, is

14

sometimes said to be benched (see dugout).

box score   A standardized digest of a game. Box scores are usually printed in newspapers on the day following the game. A box score tells the outcome of the game and how individual players did and outlines how the game went inning by inning.

Abbreviations in a Box Score

ab—at-bats
r—runs
h—hits
bi—(runs) batted in
dp—double plays
lob—(runners) left on base
hr—home runs
sb—stolen bases
s—sacrifices
sf—sacrifice flies
hbp—hit by pitch
ip—innings pitched
w—winning pitcher
l—losing pitcher
r—runs
er—earned runs
bb—bases on balls
so—strikeouts
2b—double
3b—triple
dh—designated hitter

---

bunt   A batted ball that is tapped softly into the infield. A bunt is properly produced when the batter moves one hand up toward the middle of the bat and pushes the ball towards the ground. Richard "Dicky" Pearce is credited with inventing this type of hit in 1866 (see illustration of batter squared around to bunt, page 16).

called game   A game that, for any reason, is suspended or ended by the umpire-in-chief.

catch   The act of taking possession of a batted or thrown ball before it touches the ground. A fielder must hold on to the ball long enough to prove he has control of it before releasing it.

catcher   The fielder behind home plate. It is his duty to catch the pitches thrown by the pitcher. The catcher works in an area designated as the catcher's box (see illustration of batter squared around to bunt).

dead ball   A ball out of play. A ball hit into the stands in foul territory is considered dead.

defensive team The team on the field. The defensive team consists of nine players: the pitcher, catcher, first baseman, second baseman, third baseman, short-stop, left fielder, center fielder, and right fielder.

designated hitter A hitter who bats in place of the pitcher in the batting order. The designated hitter rule was adopted by the American League in 1973, but it has yet to be adopted by the National League. The National League teams, however, use the tenth man in the lineup during the World Series every other year.

double A batted ball in fair territory that allows the hitter to reach second base safely.

doubleheader Two games played by the same teams on the same day (see **triple-header**).

double play A defensive play in which two base runners are put out or tagged out in succession provided that no errors occur between putouts. The most common double play in baseball happens when a runner is on first base and the batter hits a sharp ground ball to the shortstop. The shortstop fields the ball and throws it to the second baseman who steps on the bag to force the advancing runner and then tosses the ball to the first baseman who puts out the hitter. Double plays can occur in many other ways (see **force play, force double play** and, in slang section, **around the horn**).

dugout At the sides of the base-ball field are enclosures, usually sunk slightly below the level of the playing field, where players stay when they are not on the field, at bat, or on base. These enclosures are the dugouts. The bench is in the dugout.

error A misplay made by a fiel-der that allows a batter to prolong his stay at the plate or reach base or that allows a base runner to advance (see **passed ball** and, in slang section, **wild pitch**).

fair territory That part of the playing field within the first and third base foul lines, from home plate to the outfield fences. A ball that is batted within this area is designated a fair ball. A ball that hits the foul line or the foul pole is within fair territory and is treated as a fair ball.

fielder A member of the defen-sive team.

fielder's choice If there is more than one runner on the base paths, an infielder, after fielding a ground ball, may choose which runner to throw or tag out. Such a play is a fielder's choice. *Example:* There are runners at first and second. The shortstop fields a ground ball and tags out the runner advancing to third. This is scored as a fielder's choice. Though the batter reaches first base safely, he is not credited with a hit.

force play   An out made by an infielder when, having clear possession of the baseball, he touches a base and does not have to tag the runner. The runner is forced to go to that base because another runner is advancing to the previous base.   *Example:* A runner is on first base. The batter hits a ball to the second baseman. The second baseman merely has to step on second base to force out the runner who is running from first (see **out**).

forfeited game   If a team violates the rules, the umpire-in-chief may end the game and declare a forfeit. The score of a forfeited game is 9–0.

foul ball   A batted ball that lands in foul territory. Foul territory lies outside the first and third base foul lines (see illustration of baseball field, pages 34–35). If a fielder touches a batted ball in foul territory and knocks it back into fair territory, the ball remains a foul ball.

foul poles   Poles, usually brightly colored, in the outfield or outfield stands indicating the boundaries for home runs. These poles are really fair poles because a batted ball that hits one of the poles is a fair ball.

foul tip   A ball that is touched by the hitter's bat but which goes straight back into the catcher's mitt. All foul tips are strikes, but on a third strike, the catcher must hold on to the ball long enough to prove he has control of it for a strikeout to be called. If the catcher drops the foul tip on the third strike, the batter continues his time at bat.

home run   A batted ball in fair territory that allows the hitter to round first, second, and third bases and reach home safely (see **grand slam** in slang section).

home team   The team whose playing field is the site of the game. The home team, often dressed in white uniforms, takes the field first and bats at the bottom of each inning. The visiting team, often dressed in gray or off-white uniforms, comes to bat at the top of each inning. *Example:* The New York Yankees play the Detroit Tigers in Detroit. The Tigers are the home team and the Yankees are the visiting team.

In baseball, because players know their home field so well, there is quite often a home team or home field advantage, and a team will probably win more games at home than on the road.

In games played on neutral

18

grounds, who will be the home team and who will be the visiting team is often decided by the flip of a coin.

illegal hit A hit made by a batter when he has one or both feet outside the batter's box.

illegal pitch A pitch not sanctioned by the official rules of baseball. *Example:* The catcher throws the ball back to the pitcher who immediately throws it back across the plate. The pitch, called a quick pitch, is illegal (see **balk** and, in slang section, see **spitball**).

infielder The first, second, or third baseman, the shortstop (the catcher or the pitcher may be considered infielders for the infield fly rule).

infield fly rule A rule that protects runners on base from being trapped. In baseball's first years, an infielder could deliberately drop a fly ball hit to the infield and easily force out runners. Hence, the infield fly rule was quickly adopted. When there are less than two outs, with runners at first and second or at first, second, and third, and the batter hits a fly ball that can be caught by one of the infielders, the umpire calls "infield fly" and the batter is automatically out.

inning One of the nine periods of play of a regulation baseball game. When the visiting team has been to bat and has committed three outs, one half inning has been played. When the home team comes to bat and commits three outs, the entire inning has been completed. To preclude ties, extra innings are added to the ordinary nine. On May 1, 1920, the Brooklyn Dodgers and the Boston Braves played a twenty-six–inning game at Ebbets Field; the score, however, remained at 1–1.

interference An act by a batter, fielder, umpire, or spectator that hinders or impedes play. *Example:* A player belts what looks like a sure triple. While the runner is rounding first base and the fielder is chasing down the ball, a spectator runs onto the field and grabs the ball. This is obvious interference, and the umpire awards the runner as many bases as he would have advanced had there been no interference.

league A group of teams that play each other during a season. In major league baseball, there are two leagues—the National League, the older of the two, and the American League.

line drive A sharply hit ball that travels on a fairly direct line from the batter to a fielder.

major league teams The teams that belong to either the National

19

or American Leagues. The current major league teams are

American League East

Baltimore Orioles
Boston Red Sox
Cleveland Indians
Detroit Tigers
Milwaukee Brewers
New York Yankees
Toronto Blue Jays

National League East

Chicago Cubs
Montreal Expos
New York Mets
Philadelphia Phillies
Pittsburgh Pirates
St. Louis Cardinals

American League West

California Angels
Chicago White Sox
Kansas City Royals
Minnesota Twins
Oakland A's
Seattle Mariners
Texas Rangers

National League West

Atlanta Braves
Cincinnati Reds
Houston Astros
Los Angeles Dodgers
San Diego Padres
San Francisco Giants

manager   The person responsible for the team during a game. All teams must be represented by a manager, and the manager may be a player or a non-player. Typical duties of a manager include selecting a lineup, deciding on pitching changes, formulating strategy, and sending in pinch hitters and pinch runners.

offensive team   The team at bat. In the American League, the team at bat uses a designated hitter. In the National League, the pitcher bats for himself.

official scorer   The person, appointed by the league president, who sits in the press box and compiles the official record of the game (see **box score**). The official scorer, not the umpires, credits hits, assists, errors.

out   Both teams have three outs per inning. A player can be put out many different ways. Some of these ways are the following:

1) a batter can strike out;
2) a batter can fly out;
3) a batter can foul out;
4) a batter can hit a ground ball and be thrown out;
5) a runner can be tagged out; and
6) a player can be called out for interference.

outfielder   Any one of the three players who play beyond the infield. These are right fielder, center fielder, and left fielder.

passed ball   A ball thrown by the pitcher that should be stopped by the catcher but which gets by him, thereby allowing a base runner to advance (see illustration, page 28).

pinch hitter   A hitter who is substituted for another batter already in the lineup. History credits Cleveland Spiders player Johnny Doyle with being the first pinch hitter.

pinch runner   A player who comes into the game to run for another player already on base. In 1974 and 1975, Oakland A's owner Charles O. Finley added to his team roster a "designated runner," Herb Washington, whose sole task was to run for men on base.

20

pitch A ball thrown to the batter by the pitcher.

pitcher The defensive player who delivers pitches to the batters.

pitcher's plate See **rubber**.

play ball or **play** The cry of the umpire to start or resume the game.

relief pitcher A pitcher brought into the game to replace the pitcher already on the mound. The relief pitcher can be credited with winning, losing, or saving a game. Hoyt Wilhelm won 123 games, lost 102, and saved 227 in relief during his career.

reverse force double play A double play in which the first out is a force play and the second out is a tag-out. The most common reverse force double play occurs when there is a runner on first base and the batter hits a ground ball to the first baseman. The first baseman steps on first to retire the batter (the force play) and then throws to the second baseman who tags the advancing runner. Once the force play is made, the second runner, however, need not advance.

rookie A baseball player in his first full season of play. Each year both the National and American leagues confer a Rookie of the Year award. In the American League, some of the recipients of

the Rookie of the Year award are Herb Score (1955), Tony Oliva (1964), Lou Piniella (1969), Fred Lynn (1975), and Paul Molitor (1978). In the National League, a few of the winners include Willie Mays (1951), Pete Rose (1963), Tom Seaver (1967), Johnny Bench (1968), and Bob Horner (1978).

rubber Also known as the pitcher's plate, the rubber is a piece of whitened rubber twenty-four inches long and six inches wide on the pitcher's mound. The pitcher must keep one foot on this plate when he is delivering a pitch to the batter, but he must take his foot off the rubber when attempting to pick a runner off base. Otherwise a balk is called. The distance from the rubber to the rear point of home plate is sixty feet six inches.

run A score made by an offensive player as he safely touches home plate after he has touched first, second, and third bases.

run down An effort made by the fielders to tag out a runner who is trapped between bases.

sacrifice A deliberate out made by the batter in order to advance a base runner. A sacrifice is not counted as a time at bat for the batter.

sacrifice fly A fly ball deliberately hit to the outfield so that a base runner may advance.

safe   The cry made by an umpire to notify a runner or fielder that the runner has made it to a base without making out.

scoreboard   A board at a playing field that gives the score of the game inning by inning. Scoreboards often relay other information to the fans, such as the scores of other games in progress, whether a given pitch is a ball or a strike, the number of the batter at bat.

single   A hit that entitles the batter to take first base.

slide   A slide occurs when a base runner drops to the dirt and skids either feet first or head first into the bag in order to avoid being tagged out (see illustration, pages 26–27).

squeeze play   A strategy used by managers to get a runner home from third base. With a runner at third, the batter attempts to squeeze the runner home by laying down a bunt, usually toward the first base side.

strike   A pitch that falls within the strike zone and is not hit by the batter or a pitch that is swung at by the batter and not hit into fair territory. With less than two strikes, a foul ball or foul tip is

22

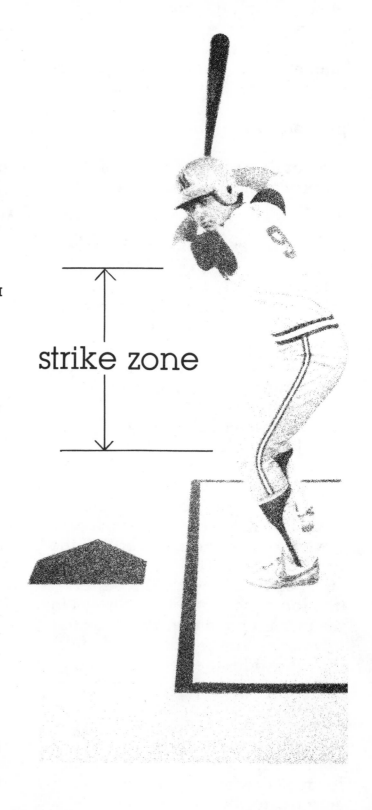

strike zone

counted as a strike. A batter has three strikes before making out.

strike zone The area over home plate between the batter's knees and armpits (in the batter's natural stance) in which any pitch is a strike. (see illustration, page 22).

suspended game An incomplete game, stopped by the umpire-in-chief, which will be completed at a later date. An extra inning game, for instance, may be suspended in order to satisfy a curfew.

tagging the runner A runner may be tagged out by an infielder if the infielder is in possession of the ball and touches the runner with the ball before the runner touches a base.

trapped ball A fly ball that is not cleanly caught by a fielder but is trapped between his glove and the ground. A trapped ball does not constitute an out, and the ball remains in play, allowing the runner to advance at his own risk.

triple A batted ball in fair territory that allows the hitter to reach third base safely.

triple-header Three games played by the same teams on the same day. There have been three

24

triple-headers played in the history of major league baseball. The last triple-header was played on October 2, 1920, between Cincinnati and Pittsburgh.

triple play A defensive play in which three base runners are put out or tagged out in succession without any errors occurring between putouts. In modern baseball history, only eight *unassisted* triple plays have been made. On July 29, 1968, Ronald Hansen, shortstop for the Washington Senators, made a triple play. With runners on first and second base, the batter, Joe Azcue of Cleveland, hit a sharp liner to Hansen, which he caught (one out). Hansen stepped on second to force the runner who had started for third (two out), and then Hansen tagged out the runner who was going into second (three out).

wild pitch A pitch that is so far outside the strike zone that the catcher cannot stop it or block it.

II. Some Baseball Slang

ace A star pitcher (remember that in 1845 runs were called aces).

around-the-horn A double play from the third baseman to the second baseman to the third baseman.

Baltimore chop A ball batted straight down so that it takes a high bounce over a fielder's head.

beanball A pitched ball thrown at the head of a batter. This pitch is illegal and very dangerous.

bingle Single.

bleachers The cheapest seats in a baseball park. They are in direct sunlight, and the fans get bleached.

bull pen An area, usually behind the outfield fence, where pitchers warm up or get ready to come into the game.

can of corn A high, lazy fly ball that is easily caught.

fan A true rooter or follower of a given team. Short for fanatic.

grand slam A home run with three men on base.

hot corner Third base.

iron mike The mechanical pitching machine used in practice.

keystone sack Second base.

rain check If a baseball game is cancelled because of rain, the fans at the ball park will be issued a stub allowing them admission to a

25

28

future game. This stub is called a rain check.

seventh-inning stretch Between halves of the seventh inning, the fans stand up, stretch their legs, refresh themselves for the final tense innings. The seventh-inning stretch has been a baseball custom for more than a hundred years.

slider A difficult pitch to hit. It is a fastball that breaks just as it crosses the plate.

spitball A pitched ball with saliva, vaseline, or other foreign substances on it to make the ball dip or jump. Sometimes called a spitter. This is an illegal pitch in modern day baseball, though some pitchers have been known to throw it.

texas leaguer A short fly ball that falls between the infield and the outfield.

tools of ignorance The catcher's equipment—a slur on catchers!

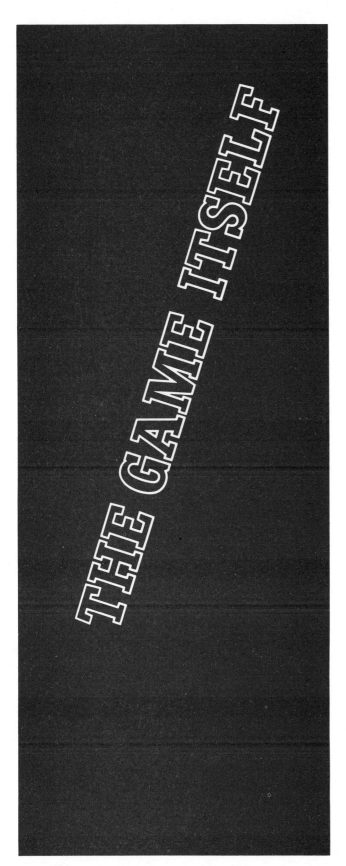

THE GAME ITSELF

I. The Objectives of the Game

A baseball game takes place between two opposing teams traditionally composed of nine players. One team takes the field while the other team bats. The object of the game is for one team, during nine innings of play, to score more runs than the other. Under certain circumstances a regulation game may consist of less than nine innings (if called by rain, say) though never less than four and one-half innings of play (see **inning** and **run** in vocabulary section).

SCORING

One run is scored when a runner legally proceeds from his batting position to first, second, and third bases and then to home plate. Each base must be touched in order. Any part of the runner's body may be used to legally touch a base including home plate. Except as explained below, the runner scores if he touches home plate before the third out is made.

A run, however, is not scored even when the runner from third base touches home plate before the third out if on the same play the batter is thrown out at first base, if there is a force at any base, or if a preceding runner is called out for missing a base.

A run does not score if the runner does not touch home plate. As an example, with the bases loaded in the last half of the ninth or extra inning, if a runner is forced home by any circumstance, including a walk or hit batter, the game is not over until the runner from third base has touched home plate and the batter has touched first base. When the runners are prevented from reaching base by a crowd which spills on to the field, the umpire awards the runners the bases that they were attempting to reach.

When a runner is forced home but refuses to touch home plate, the umpire, after a reasonable length of time, calls the runner out. The run does not count, and the game continues. With bases loaded and two out, if the batter is awarded but refuses to touch first base, the batter is called out, the run does not count, and the game continues. With fewer than two outs, the batter is out if he refuses to touch first base, but the run scores.

Once a run has scored within the rules, it cannot be cancelled. For example, a run counts despite the return of the runner to third base because he mistakenly believed he had left third base early (before a fly ball was caught).

The batting team, the offense, is retired and becomes the team in the field when any combination of three of its batters or runners are put out. The team in the field, the defense, becomes the offensive team when the batting team is retired.

II. The Playing Field

To best understand what the playing field of a baseball park looks like, turn to the diagrams on pages 34–36.

The infield is a square measuring 90 feet per side. By extending the foul line on the first and third base sides of the infield, we determine the playing area of the outfield. From ball park to ball park, however, there are considerable differences between the distances from home plate to the nearest fence. Official baseball rules dictate that the distance from home plate to the nearest fence or other obstruction on fair territory shall be at least 250 feet. The distance from home plate to the center field stands or fence is usually in the neighborhood of four hundred feet. Tiger Stadium, home of the Detroit Tigers in the American League, has the following measurements: 325 feet along the first base side; 340 feet along the third base line; 440 feet from home plate to the deepest part of center field.

THE INFIELD

The pitcher's plate must be ten inches above the level of home plate. The infield must be graded so that home plate and the base lines are level.

The distance from home plate to second base is 127 feet and three and three-eighths inches (measurements made from home plate are taken from that point where the third and first base lines intersect).* The distance from home plate to first base measures 90 feet. The distance from first base to second base measures 90 feet. The distance from second base to third base measures 90 feet. The distance between first base and third base measures 127 feet and three and three-eighths inches.

The distance from home plate to the back stop should be at least 60 feet.

*An imaginary line from home plate through the pitcher's plate to second base should run in an east-northeast direction.

The distance from the baselines to the nearest grandstand or seating area or fence or any other obstruction should be at least 60 feet.

Foul lines and all other playing lines on the field are indicated by chalk, wet lime, or any other white substance that will not interfere with play (see diagrams on pages 34–37 for the layout of the batter's box, the catcher's box, the coaches' boxes, and so on).

HOME BASE

What the average fan calls home plate is actually a five-sided slab of whitened rubber. Two edges of this marker are twelve inches long, one edge is seventeen inches long, and the two short edges are eight and one-half inches long.

The two twelve-inch sides of home plate are set on the ground in such a way as to coincide with the third and first base lines. The seventeen-inch edge faces the pitcher's mound.

This home plate, with its top edges beveled, is to be set at ground level.

THE BASES

The bases are marked by white canvas bags filled with soft material. These bags are fifteen inches square, and they are between three and five inches thick. These bags, indicating first base, second base, and third base, are securely attached to the ground in fair terri-

33

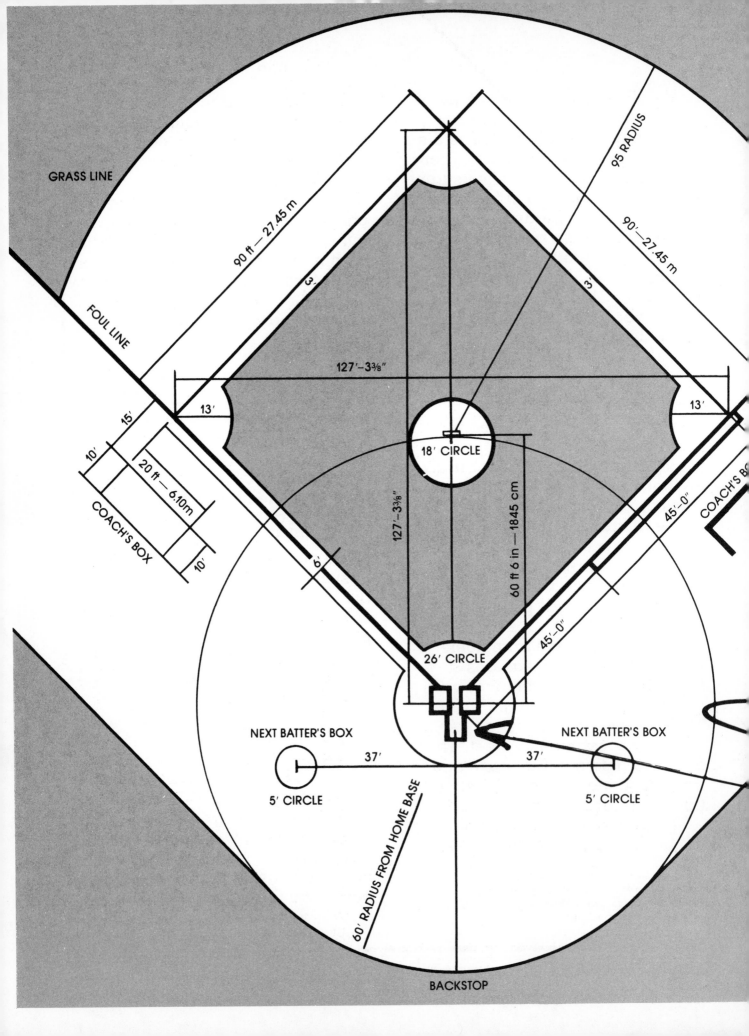

GRASS LINE

FOUL LINE

90 ft — 27.45 m

3'

95 RADIUS

90'—27.45 m

3'

127'–3⅜"

13'

13'

15'

10'

20 ft — 6.10m

COACH'S BOX

10'

18' CIRCLE

127'–3⅜"

60 ft 6 in — 1845 cm

45'–0"

COACH'S BOX

6'

26' CIRCLE

45'–0"

NEXT BATTER'S BOX

37'

NEXT BATTER'S BOX

37'

5' CIRCLE

5' CIRCLE

60' RADIUS FROM HOME BASE

BACKSTOP

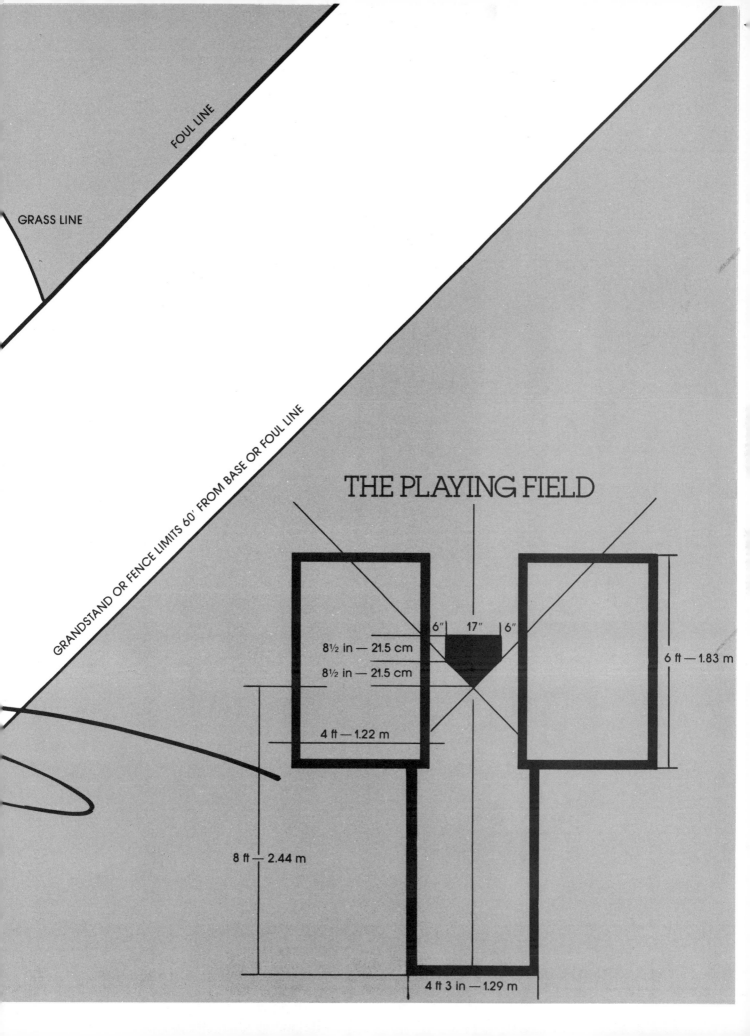

FOUL LINE

GRASS LINE

GRANDSTAND OR FENCE LIMITS 60' FROM BASE OR FOUL LINE

THE PLAYING FIELD

6" 17" 6"

8½ in — 21.5 cm

8½ in — 21.5 cm

6 ft — 1.83 m

4 ft — 1.22 m

8 ft — 2.44 m

4 ft 3 in — 1.29 m

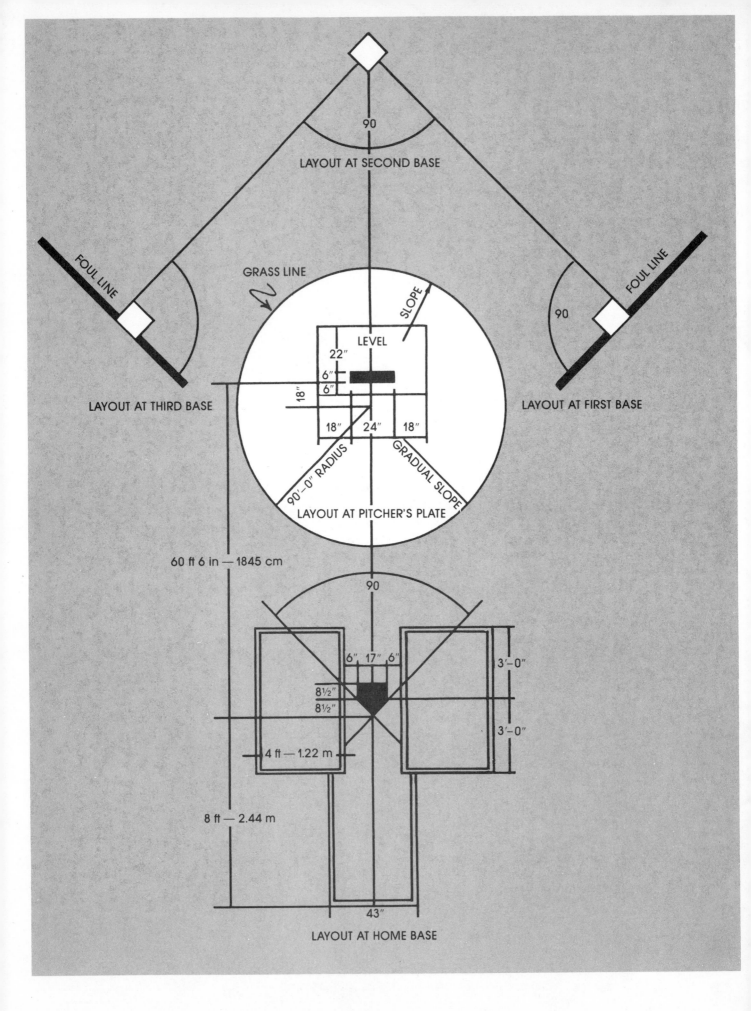

LAYOUT AT SECOND BASE

FOUL LINE

GRASS LINE

SLOPE

LEVEL

22"

6"

6"

18"

18" 24" 18"

90'–0" RADIUS

GRADUAL SLOPE

LAYOUT AT THIRD BASE

FOUL LINE

90

LAYOUT AT FIRST BASE

LAYOUT AT PITCHER'S PLATE

60 ft 6 in — 1845 cm

90

6" 17" 6"

3'–0"

8½"

8½"

3'–0"

4 ft — 1.22 m

8 ft — 2.44 m

43"

LAYOUT AT HOME BASE

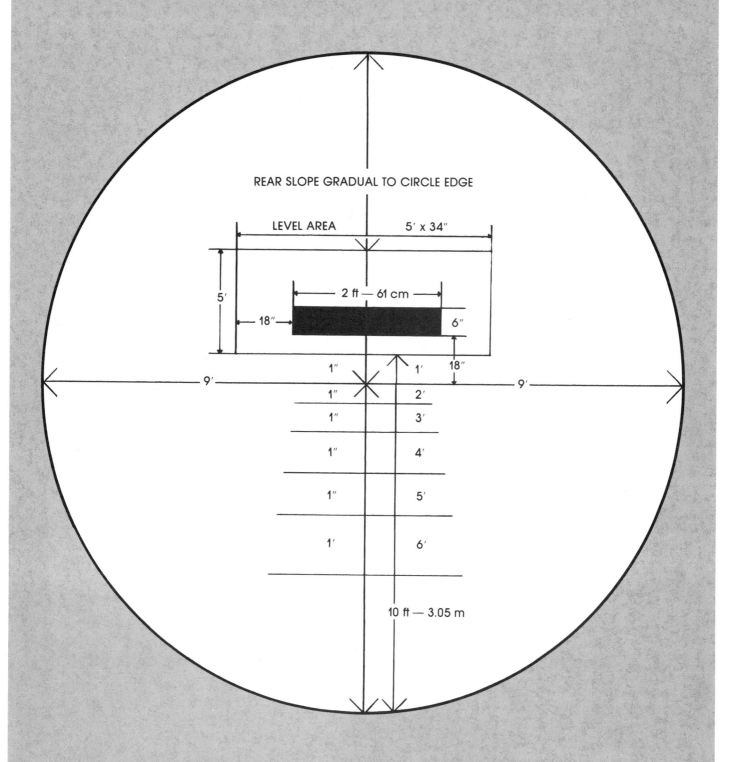

THE PITCHING MOUND

tory and completely within the infield.

Lights come within the jurisdiction of the chief umpire. He determines when playing field lights should be turned on in order to avoid hazards caused by darkness.

III. The Equipment

THE BASEBALL
The official baseball is a sphere manufactured by winding yarn around a tiny core of cork or rubber. The yarn is then covered with two strips of white horsehide or cowhide. The two strips are tightly sewn. This white sphere, upon which everything in the game depends, measures between nine and nine and one-quarter inches in circumference and weighs between five and five and one-quarter ounces avoirdupois. If a ball weighs more than five and one-quarter ounces, it cannot be used.

There is much discussion in baseball circles about whether today's baseball is too lively. There is no doubt, however, that more home runs are being hit today than ever before. In 1902, for example, Tommy Leach of the Pittsburgh Pirates led the National League in home runs, and he was able to hit only six!

38

Although Oakland A's owner Charles O. Finley once tried to introduce an orange-tinted baseball into the game, all official baseballs must be white.*

THE BAT
The bat is a rounded stick or club used to hit the baseball. Official baseball bats, usually made from a single piece of solid wood,† must not measure more than two

*A yellow baseball was used in the April 27, 1938, Columbia-Fordham game.
†A bat may also be made from a block of wood consisting of two pieces of bonded wood, provided the grain direction is parallel to the length of the bat.

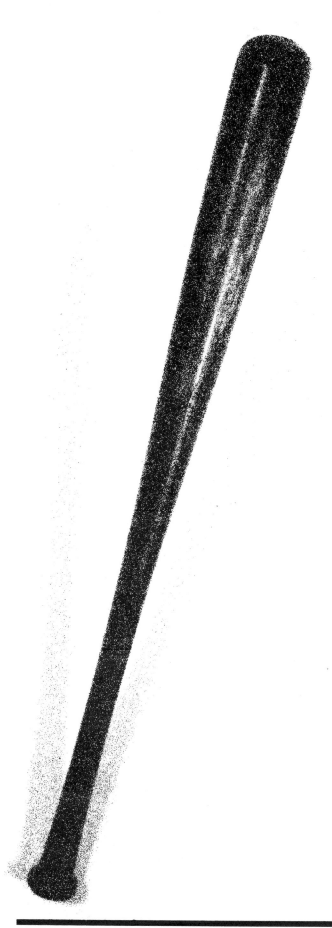

and three-quarter inches in diameter and must be no more than forty-two inches in length. Bats must be of a natural wood color. No colored bats are permitted in official games unless such bats are approved by the rules committee of major league baseball.

A player may improve the grip of his bat by covering the handle with any material he chooses—pine tar is, perhaps, the most common substance used for such a purpose—provided that any material used on the handle does not extend for more than eighteen inches from the end of the bat.

Until 1893, it was permissible for a portion of the bat to be flat, but today's bats must be round, though a player is allowed to cup his bat, that is, make a slight indentation on the end of his bat. This indentation, however, may not be greater than one inch in depth, nor can it be wider than two inches. Its diameter may be no less than one inch.

There is no weight restriction on bats. A softball bat, however, may weigh no more than thirty-eight ounces and may be made of metal.

THE GLOVES

The First Baseman's Glove.* The glove worn by the first baseman

*The first first baseman to wear a glove was Charles Waite of Boston in 1875. The glove had a large opening at the back for ventilation and was flesh colored so it would not be noticed. When it was noticed, fans and teammates called Waite a sissy!

should not be more than eight inches wide across the palm nor more than twelve inches long. The web of the glove measures no more than five inches from the base of the thumb to the top.

There is no weight limitation on the first baseman's glove.

The Gloves of Other Fielders. The gloves may not be more than seven and three-quarter inches wide nor more than twelve inches from the heel of the glove through the pocket to the tip of any one of the fingers.

The space between the first finger and the thumb of these gloves is known as the crotch. This space may be filled with a backstop of leather webbing, but the webbing of the crotch may not be laced in such a manner that it makes a netlike trap. (This restriction also applies to first basemen's gloves.)

The crotch of the glove, not measuring more than four and one-half inches high, five and three-quarter inches deep, and three and one-half inches wide at the bottom, must be attached to the body of the glove by leather lacing. There is no restriction on the weight of the glove.

The Pitcher's Glove. The glove of the pitcher must be of one color, but the color may not be white or gray. No material of a different color can be attached to the pitcher's glove.

40

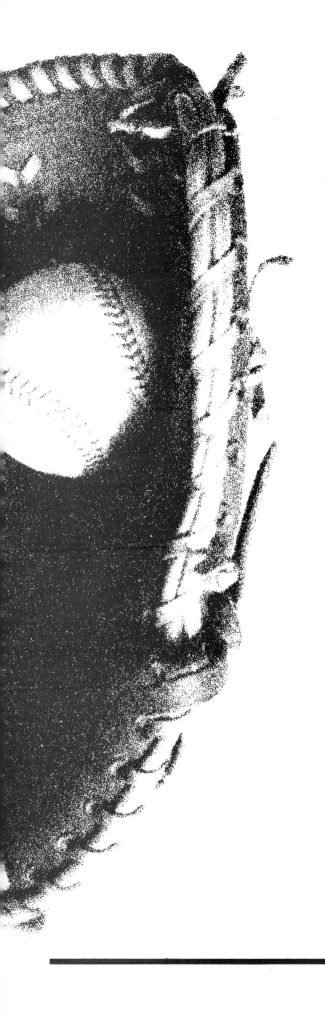

41

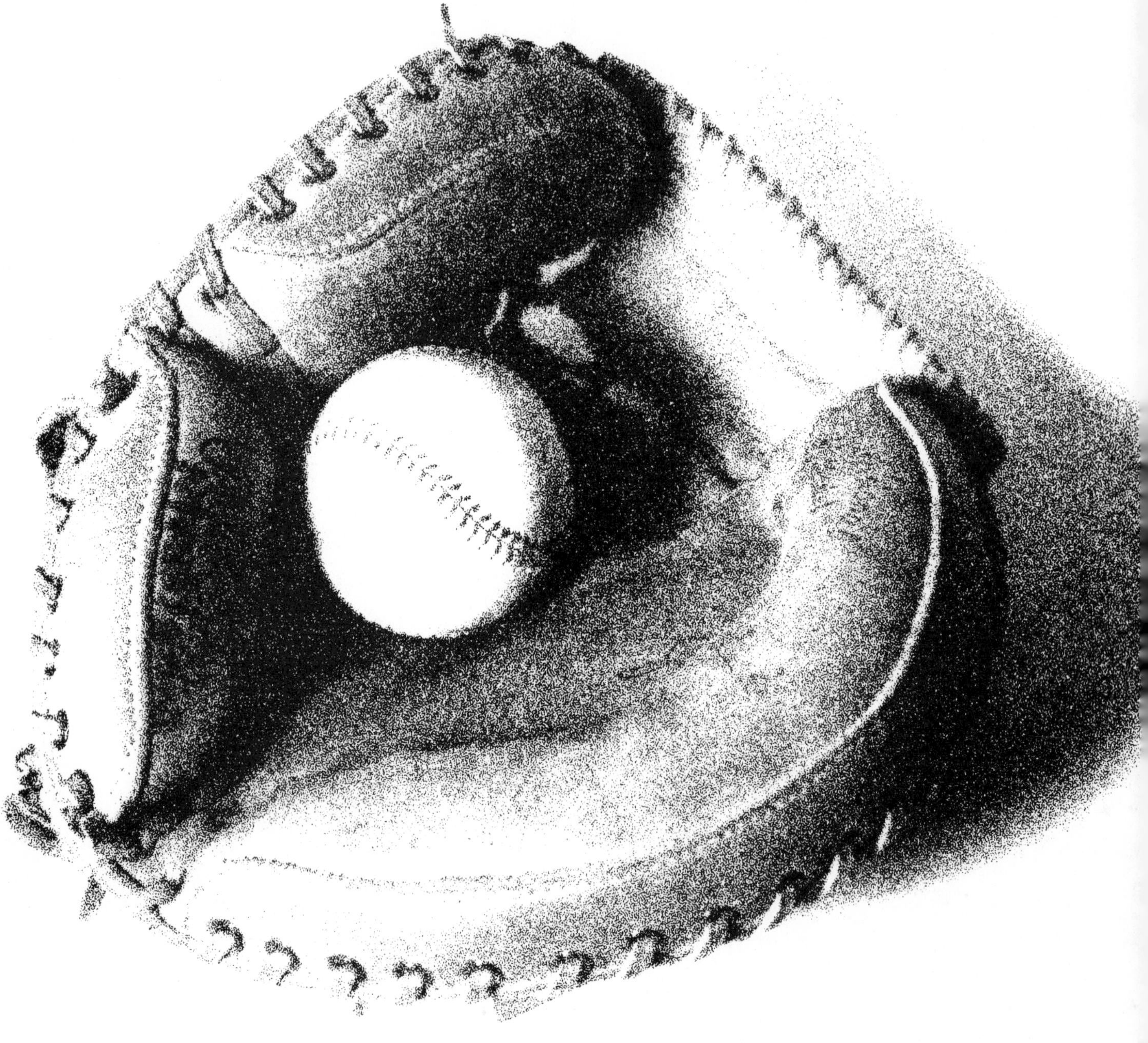

HELMETS

No player is allowed to bat unless he wears some type of protective helmet. Such helmets must have earflaps.* A player who refuses to wear a helmet while at bat is ejected from the game.

*Players in the major leagues when the earflap rule was adopted were exempt from using the mandatory flaps.

44

catcher's protective gear

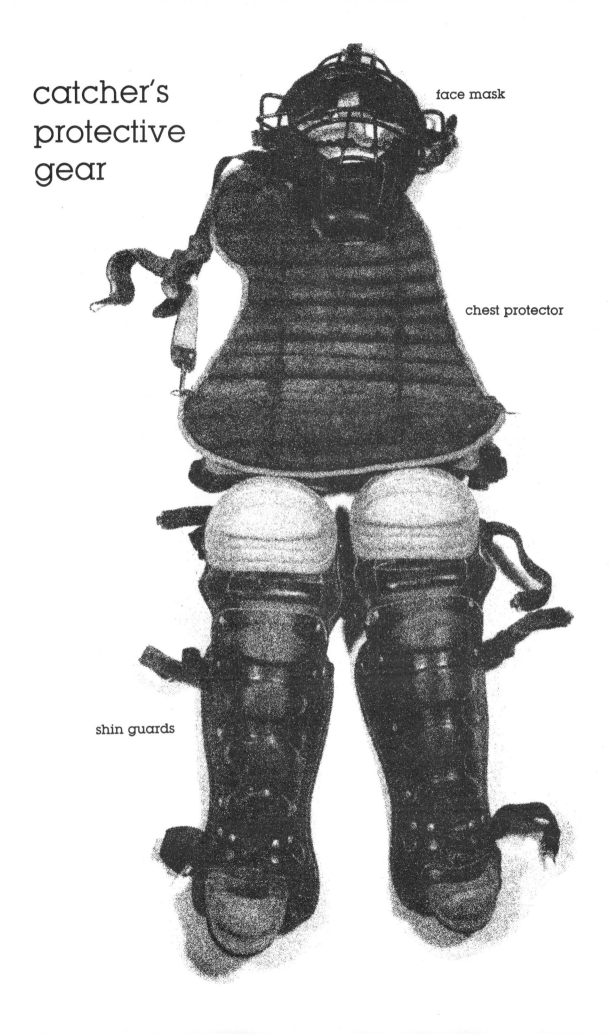

face mask

chest protector

shin guards

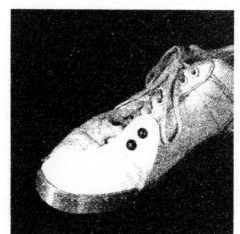

toe plate

IV. Before the Game Begins

Before a baseball game starts, the umpire-in-chief makes certain that all rules pertaining to the equipment of the game and pertaining to the behavior of the manager, coaches, and players are strictly enforced.

The umpire-in-chief checks that all the white playing lines are clearly marked and that the playing field itself is laid out according to the rules.

While in uniform, players on opposing teams are not allowed to fraternize. While in uniform, players are not allowed to sit in the stands nor to fraternize with spectators.

A. CHECKING THE BASEBALLS

The home team supplies all the baseballs used in the game. Such baseballs must be of regulation size and weight and material, and each baseball must be in a sealed package. Each sealed package carries the signature of the league president. Right before game time, the umpire-in-chief opens each package and makes certain that the gloss is removed from each baseball.

At least twelve regulation baseballs must be available at all times to be put into play as needed. Once the game begins, the umpire-in-chief carries at all times on his person at least two

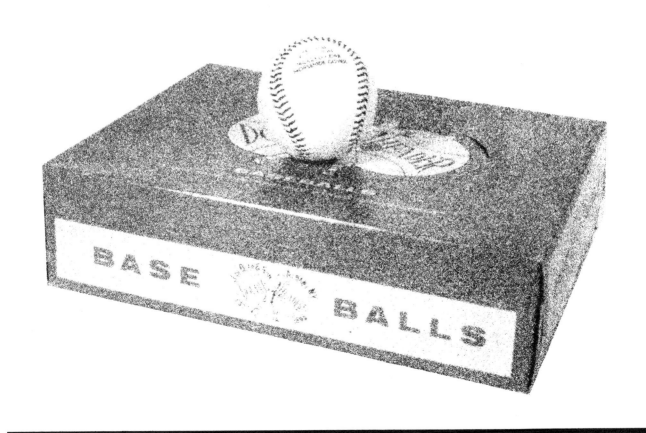

baseballs. New baseballs are put into play

1) when a baseball becomes scuffed, discolored, or generally unfit for play;
2) when the pitcher requests a new ball; and
3) when a ball is hit into the stands.

B. JUDGING THE WEATHER

The manager of the home team decides whether or not a game shall be delayed because of bad weather or because of unfit playing conditions.

The above rule, however, is not applicable to second games of doubleheaders. Once the first game of a doubleheader has been played, the umpire-in-chief determines whether or not the second game will be played.

V. The Game Begins

The management of the home team decides whether the game begins on time, is delayed, or is postponed. Five minutes before the announced starting time, the chief umpire proceeds to home plate. Managers of the opposing teams meet the chief umpire at home plate and submit to him two copies of their batting orders. The umpire then checks the batting orders for accuracy and keeps one copy of each. The umpire's copies are the official ones. Managers of the opposing teams are given verified copies of the other team's batting order. Once the umpire accepts the batting orders, there can, under the rules, be no changes except for substitutions. Substitutes take the place in the batting order of the players they replace. The umpire, however, checks the batting orders for technical errors; for instance, too few or too many players or confusing names. His object is to ensure that innocent clerical mistakes will not influence the course of the game.

TAKING THE FIELD

As soon as the umpire receives the batting order from the home team, he alone controls the continuation of play as it may be affected by weather or other playing conditions. The game begins when the home team takes the field, the first visiting batter gets into the batter's box, and the umpire says play. Upon call of play, all fielders except the catcher, who is right behind home plate, must be in fair ground.

The catcher's normal position is directly behind home plate. He may move from his position to catch a pitch or a thrown or batted ball. When the batter is offered an intentional walk, the catcher must remain within the catcher's box until the pitcher releases the ball. If the catcher leaves his box too early, the pitcher is called for a balk.

The pitcher while pitching must be in contact with the rubber.

After the ball has been put into play, no player on the batting team except the batter or a runner approaching home plate from third base may legally enter the catcher's box.

COACHES

There may be no more than two coaches on the field for the team at bat. They work from the coaches' boxes near first and third bases. If they work outside the limits of the coaches' boxes, upon complaint by the manager of the team in the field, coaches of both teams are directed by the umpire to stay within the coaching boxes throughout the entire game. Coaches who fail to obey this rule are expelled from the game and removed from the playing field. A coach, however, may leave his box to direct a running play before him if he does not in any way interfere with the action of the game.

PLAY BEGINS

The ball is put into play by the pitcher when he pitches to home plate. The batter may or may not swing at the pitch. After a dead ball, when the pitcher again steps on the rubber with the ball, the umpire behind home plate calls play. Batters, the offense, seek to become runners and eventually to score, while the defense, the

49

pitcher, catcher, and fielders, seeks to keep batters off the bases and to stop runners from scoring.

VI. Dead Ball

If the following circumstances occur, the ball is dead, play stops, and the runners *may not* advance and must return to base: when a ball is batted contrary to the rules (for example, a batter hits a pitch while out of the batter's box); when a batted ball is called foul and is not caught on the fly by a fielder (play does not continue until each runner has returned to the base he started from); when the umpire behind home plate interferes with the catcher's throw to any fielder including the pitcher (unless the catcher is able to throw out a runner, then the runner is out despite the umpire's interference).

If the following circumstances occur the ball is dead, play stops, but the runner or runners *may* advance one base: when the pitcher balks; when a batter's body or clothing is hit by a pitch while the batter is legally within the batter's box (all runners on base advance only if forced by the award of first base to the batter); and when a legal pitch hits a runner approaching home plate.

When a batted ball hits a runner or umpire in fair ground before the ball touches the pitcher or any infielder, the ball is dead. If a batted ball touches an umpire before it passes any infielder except the pitcher, the ball is also dead. If a batted ball touches an umpire in the infield after the ball has passed the pitcher, it is dead.

A batted ball which rebounds from a fielder in fair ground, hits a runner or umpire, and then is caught by an infielder is still in play despite the fact that the ball never touched the ground (if the batter reaches first base before he is put out by a tag or throw, he is safe).

When a batted ball in fair ground passes by an infielder and hits a runner right behind that infielder, the ball is in play (if the ball was not playable by any other infielder, the runner may advance and is not considered out).

If an umpire or base coach is accidentally hit by a thrown ball or if an umpire is hit by a pitch, the ball remains in play. The runner is out, however, if a base coach intentionally interferes with a thrown ball.

A ball which loses part or all of its cover remains in play. When the play ends, only then is the ball dead.

PITCHES
When a pitch gets by the catcher and sticks in the umpire's equipment, his mask or chest protector, the ball is dead and the runners advance one base. When an umpire is hit by a foul tip on the third

strike, the ball is dead. Even when a foul tip is caught on a fly as it bounces off the umpire or his equipment, the batter is not out. A foul tip which sticks in the umpire's equipment is also dead and cannot be called the third strike. When a catcher misses the third strike, the ball is in play if it hits the umpire. (If the ball is caught on the fly by a fielder as it bounces off the umpire, however, the batter is not out.)

TIME CALLED

Time called by any umpire stops play immediately. The ball is then dead. Time is called by an umpire when conditions on the field such as the failure of artificial lights, the fall of darkness, or bad weather warrant the stop of play.

Time is also called by an umpire when a manager asks to make a substitution or to confer with his players. The umpire calls time when he wishes to confer with anyone, remove any person from the field, or examine the condition of the baseball.

During a play, time is not called unless the playing field lights fail or a player or umpire cannot continue because of injury. A runner may substitute for an injured player who is entitled to advance, as when a home run is hit over the fence and the batter is injured before he can circle the bases.

A PLAYER FALLS INTO THE STANDS
The ball becomes dead when a fielder catches a fly ball and then falls into the stands, the dugout, or a roped-off area on the field reserved for spectators. Runners, however, may advance one base. If after a fly ball is caught, the player who caught it goes into the stands, dugout, or roped-off area and does not himself fall, the ball is live, in play, and those on base run at their own risk. A home run, however, is scored when a fielder falls or leaps into the stands with a ball caught just as it was going over the outfield fence in fair territory.

DEAD BALLS AND SCORING
During the time that a ball is dead, runners may not score, advance, or be put out. Even when the ball is dead, however, the umpire may award runners additional bases. For example, runners may advance on a dead ball when a ball is overthrown, the pitcher balks, a fielder interferes with a runner or when a batter has hit a home run over the fence or a ground rule double.

VII. Umpiring

JURISDICTION
At least one umpire shall be designated by the league president to serve during each official game. All games which are counted for the record are entitled "championship games". The umpires shall interpret the rules. They are the sole judges of balls and strikes, fair or foul, and out or safe. They shall also determine when a ball is dead (time out) and when it is alive (in play). The umpire shall also adjudge if games once begun shall be suspended or called because of weather or other poor playing conditions.

The rules shall govern and so be applied by the umpires. When a situation does not fall within the stated rules, the umpire is fully empowered to enforce his own policy or decision. Umpires may not be removed from authority during a game without medical justification.

THE POWER TO EJECT
The umpire represents the league. He has the right and the duty to keep order and require compliance with all league and game rules. An umpire is empowered to direct or prohibit the specific performance of any team official or employee as well as players, managers, and coaches in order to uphold and carry out the rules.

Every umpire may bar from further participation in the game and from the field itself any manager, coach, player, or reserve player for unsportsmanlike conduct, including language, or for criticizing an umpire's decision. When a player is barred during the course of a play, the player barred may continue until that play is fully completed.

Any person without authority to be on the playing field, or in the dugouts or bull pens may be barred from the field by the umpire. The umpire may bar for cause those persons who are authorized to be on the field, such as media crews, groundskeepers, and ushers.

ONE UMPIRE

When only one umpire is available, he shall have complete control and may not delegate his authority. He shall be the judge of where to station himself. At his

discretion, he may elect to stand behind the pitcher with runners on base. In most situations, however, a lone umpire will station himself behind the catcher.

THE CHIEF UMPIRE

A chief umpire shall be named for each game in which there is more than one umpire. He is also called the plate umpire. The plate umpire shall assume complete control of the game. He shall assure that rules are honored and correct demeanor is upheld. He is the sole judge of whether or not a game is to be forfeited.

Before a game, the chief umpire shall report if there is any applicable time limit and, if so, the precise time of that limit. He may inform the public of any exceptional ground rules. He is required to notify the official scorer of the batting orders presented by the managers at the beginning of the game. If requested by the official scorer, the chief umpire shall notify him of any changes in lineups or batting orders.

The plate umpire stands behind the catcher. From that position, he shall call balls and strikes and keep the count. He is responsible for all calls involving the batter; for example, whether or not the batter is hit by a pitch. He shall determine fair or foul and all other calls not within the jurisdiction of the field umpires.

FIELD UMPIRES

As opposed to the plate umpire's fixed position behind the catcher, the umpire in the field, also called the base umpire, shall assume a position which may vary according to his judgment and the game situation. The field umpire, as well as the plate umpire, may call balks, illegal pitches, improper alteration of the ball, and time. The field umpire's jurisdiction is only limited by that which is specifically reserved for the plate umpire. The field umpire may not forfeit games, but in all other matters concerning the rules, he, as well as the plate umpire, is fully empowered to compel adherence. Both the plate and field umpires are responsible for upholding the standards of correct demeanor for players, coaches, and managers.

CONFLICTING DECISIONS

The chief umpire shall bring all umpires together after there have been differing decisions by two or more umpires on the same play. Players and managers shall be excluded from the conference. The umpires shall confer, discussing the decisions and the vantage points of the individual umpires. The chief umpire, or an umpire named by the league president for such circumstances, shall make the final decision. All other decisions shall be annulled and play shall continue.

JUDGMENT CALLS

There can be no argument over a judgment call by an umpire. Among the many judgment calls, a few examples are strikes and balls, fair or foul, and safe or out. Players, reserve players, managers, and coaches may not criticize these calls. An umpire's decision on a judgment call is final.

STRIKES AND BALLS

It is prohibited to criticize a ball or strike call. Managers, coaches, and reserve players may not leave the coaches' boxes, on-deck circles, dugouts, or bull pens to object. Fielders may not leave their positions. Runners may not leave their bases. The umpire shall warn those who head toward home plate to criticize a ball or strike call. If the warning goes unheeded, that person shall be barred from the game.

REPORT TO THE LEAGUE PRESIDENT

The chief umpire is required to notify the league president of all significant infractions of the rules and the full circumstances concerning the ejection from the game or field of any personnel. The league president is empowered to impose sanctions upon personnel ejected.

HALF SWINGS

When the plate umpire calls the pitch on which the batter makes a half swing a strike, there can be no appeal. When the pitch on the half swing is called a ball, the catcher or his manager may require the plate umpire to confer with a field umpire. Field umpires are responsible for this call when so requested by the plate umpire. After the request, field umpires shall make the call promptly. If a strike is called by the field umpire, then that pitch shall be a strike. In this circumstance, the field umpire's judgment is final.

The manager of the batting team may validly object to a plate umpire who does not request the decision of the field umpire about a half swing, but there can be no objection on the ball or strike call itself. Umpires shall not allow a manager to dispute when he seeks to argue ball or strike under cover of a debate about the half swing.

While the appeal on a half swing is being made, the ball remains in play. Runners proceed at their own risk. Thus, if the plate umpire calls a ball on a half swing, players should be aware that the situation may quickly change if the field umpire on appeal calls a strike. For example, there is a runner on first with one out and the count three balls and one strike on the batter. On the next pitch, the batter takes a half swing and the plate umpire calls a ball. The runner on first, thinking the batter has walked, begins to trot to second base. On appeal, the field umpire calls a strike and

the catcher throws to the second baseman, who tags out the runner. The runner, in the above situation, should not have anticipated the walk.

APPEALS

When he believes an umpire has misinterpreted the rules in the course of making a decision, a manager may protest that decision. He may appeal for the umpire to reverse himself, but he may only appeal to the umpire involved. That umpire, upon appeal, may, but is not compelled to, confer with the other umpires. He shall then respond to the manager's appeal.

It is improper and a violation of the rules for one umpire to object to or change in any manner the decision of another umpire without that umpire's specific request.

VIII. Pitching

WARM-UP PITCHES

A pitcher is allowed eight warm-up pitches before each inning. The warm-up pitches must be made in one minute or less and only when the ball is dead. The same number of pitches, eight, is to be given pitchers who start, pitched in the previous inning, or come in as relievers.

Relief pitchers, without sufficient warm-up, called into the game because of circumstances that could not reasonably have been foreseen, may be allowed as much warm-up time as needed. The amount of warm-up time in these instances shall be determined by the chief umpire.

THE MANAGER'S VISITS TO THE MOUND

A manager is allowed one discussion without conditions on the mound with each game pitcher during each inning. After the second such discussion in an inning, the pitcher must leave the game.

During the at-bat of one batter, a manager may not have more than one discussion with his game pitcher. If the manager continues to the mound a second time after being warned by the umpire, the manager shall be barred from the playing field. The manager may then not remain in the dugout nor have any connection with the game except that he shall have been warned to ready a relief pitcher. Because of the manager's second and illegal trip to the mound, the pitcher then in the game must continue pitching until the present batter is out or becomes a base runner. And after that batter concludes his time at bat, the pitcher is then required to leave the game.

When a substitute batter enters the game, for purposes of this rule, it shall be as if another batter is at home plate. Therefore, a manager may make a second visit in one inning to the same pitcher if a batter is substituted for before he concludes his time at bat, but following the general rule, after that visit the pitcher must leave the game.

THE MANAGER'S VISITS TO THE MOUND: DEFINITIONS

When a manager visits and holds a discussion with a defensive player who then in turn goes to the mound for a discussion with the pitcher, it shall be counted as a visit by the manager.

When a manager visits the mound and then takes out the pitcher, his discussion, if any, with the incoming relief pitcher shall be counted as a visit to that incoming pitcher.

A trip to the mound is terminated and shall count as one visit when the manager leaves the area bounded by a circle with a radius nine feet from the pitcher's plate (the rubber).

In this section on visits to the mound, *manager* is defined as *manager* or *coach*.

PITCHING REGULATIONS

The Ball. A pitcher is prohibited from altering the surface of the ball in any manner. Saliva or any other foreign substance may not be applied to the ball. No foreign substance may be in the possession of the pitcher while on the mound.

The Rosin Bag. The ball is in play if it strikes the rosin bag. Before the game starts, the chief umpire shall put the rosin bag in back of the rubber on the pitcher's mound. Each umpire is to carry a rosin bag. If the ground is wet or if it is raining, the chief umpire may direct that the rosin bag be placed in the pitcher's uniform pants pocket.

Rosin may not be applied directly to the ball, uniform, or glove by any pitcher or other player. A pitcher or other player may apply rosin directly to his hands only. He may rub up the ball with his hands with or without having first applied rosin to his hands.

61

The Pitching Motion and Delivery. The pitcher may not throw a shine, mud, emory, or spit ball. He may not spit on the ball, his glove, or hands. He may not rub the ball across his uniform, body, or glove. If, in the umpire's judgment, such an infraction takes place, the umpire is to call the pitch a ball, notify the pitcher, and announce to the spectators the nature of the infraction of the rules. A second infraction by the same pitcher during that game requires the pitcher's immediate ejection.

If, however, a pitch is delivered and the batter attains first base and other runners are not retired before advancing at least one base, the play stands. The

manager of the batting team may accept any other resultant play if he makes his intention known to the umpire as soon as the play has ended. For example, after an infraction of this rule, if a batter flied out and a runner from third scored after the catch, a manager might very well accept the play to gain the run. Despite the manager's acceptance of the play, the pitcher would, nevertheless, be subject to the penalties provided for by this rule.

The Pitcher's Hand to His Mouth. While on the mound, a pitcher may under no circumstances touch his mouth or lips with his throwing hand. If, in the umpire's judgment, such an infraction takes place, the umpire is to call a ball. If, however, a pitch is delivered and the batter attains first base and other runners are not retired before advancing at least one base, the play stands. Subsequent violations are to be referred to the league president for sanctions. As in previous circumstances, the manager of the batting team may accept any resultant play if he makes his intention known to the umpire as soon as the play has ended.

Throwing at the Batter. As soon as a pitcher has intentionally, as determined by the umpire, tried to hit a batter with a pitch, both team's managers and the pitcher shall be warned. The warning

shall state that if another pitch, by either team's pitcher, is thrown at a batter, the offending pitcher shall be ejected from the game at once. If necessary, in the opinion of the umpire, the warning may also be given at any time before the start of a game. After receiving a warning, a pitcher who throws at a batter, as determined by the umpire, must be ejected from the game.

Delay of the Game. A pitcher may not intentionally delay the game. Intentional delay includes, but is not limited to, throwing the ball, with a batter in the batter's box, to fielders, excluding the catcher, when a play on a runner is not in process. After the first such incident, the umpire shall warn the pitcher. A second such delay by the same pitcher requires his immediate ejection.

A pitcher, after the catcher returns the ball to him and when there are no runners on base, may take no longer than twenty seconds to throw to the batter. The catcher, after receiving a pitch, is required to quickly throw back to the pitcher. The pitcher is required to assume his pitching position without undue delay. The umpire shall declare a ball each time there is an unwarranted delay. The umpire, to prevent delay, shall react immediately when such tactics are open and without justification.

The Quick Pitch. When a pitcher

does not wait to pitch until the batter is substantially settled in the batter's box, a balk shall be called. When the bases are empty, the pitch, regardless of its position relative to the strike zone, shall be called a ball. The safety of players requires that the quick pitch be prevented.

Balks. A balk requires that each runner on base move ahead one base. The ball is dead except, if a pitch is delivered and the batter attains first base and the other runners on base are not retired before advancing one base, the play stands.

A balk shall be called if the pitcher drops the ball, intentionally or not, when he is on the rubber; if a pitch, during an intentional walk, is made when the catcher is not in his box; if the pitcher delays the game without cause; if the pitcher pitches while not looking toward the batter; or if an illegal pitch is delivered.

Balks on Throws to a Base. A balk shall be called when a pitcher on the rubber throws to a base without first stepping straight toward that base. Thus, a pitcher may not throw to a base by turning only his body or rotating off the foot not on the rubber. A balk shall be called when the pitcher, on the rubber, starts but does not complete a throw to first base. The pitcher need not complete a throw to second or third base.

If a pitcher fakes toward an occupied base, unless it is first base,

he need not throw and may then turn and throw to another base. If, however, he does go to another base, he must also step straight toward that base before he throws.

A pitcher, unless making a play, while on the rubber, may not start or complete a throw to a base at which there is no runner.

Balks on Pitching Motions. A balk is called if a pitcher, when not on the rubber, moves in any manner that is related to his pitching motion. When the pitcher without the ball stands on or straddling the rubber or fakes a pitch when not on the rubber, a balk shall be called.

When the pitcher does not completely stop after coming to his set position, a balk shall be called. And a balk shall also be called when a pitcher, in pitching position, takes his hand off the ball to do anything but throw to a base or pitch.

Pitching Procedure. A pitcher is required to be in contact with the rubber when he receives the catcher's sign. The pitcher may step off the rubber after he gets the sign but must hold his hands at his side as he steps off. Although a pitcher may occasionally step off the rubber after receiving the sign, he may not do so regularly. The pitcher may not quick pitch, that is, rapidly step on the rubber and deliver the ball to the batter. A pitcher may pitch from the windup or set position, but no other pitching motions are permitted.

The Windup. Prior to the windup,

a pitcher is required to stand with his pivot foot on or touching the front side of the pitcher's rubber. Thus, he must pitch from the front portion of the rubber and not from an exaggerated side angle. He may not position his pivot foot so that it touches only the side of the pitcher's rubber. His other foot may be positioned in back of the rubber. He must stand so that he faces the batter. When the pitcher is in such a position, he must also, with his glove and bare hand, hold the ball in front of him.

After he takes the windup position, he may step backward and then forward with his free foot but only as he is in the act of pitching to the batter. He may not pick up either foot for any other purpose. Once in position, any action taken by the pitcher which is related to his pitching motion requires that, without hesitation or change, he continue his motion and pitch to the batter.

In the windup position, the free foot, not the pivot foot, may be placed anywhere directly behind but not to the side of the pitcher's rubber. The pitcher may step backward and then forward with the free foot but may not in any circumstance step to the right or left of the pitcher's rubber. He must always step toward the batter.

As the pitcher stands in the windup position, he may not shift into the stretch or set position. The pitcher in the windup position has three options. He must step off the

pitcher's rubber with his hands at his sides; throw to a base, after stepping toward that base, in an effort to pick off a runner; or pitch to a batter.

Stretch and Set. A pitcher, if not in the windup position, is required to come to a set position. In this posture a pitcher is required to stand with his pivot foot on or touching the front side of the rubber. He may not position his pivot foot so that it touches only the side of the pitcher's rubber. Thus, he must pitch from the front portion of the pitcher's rubber and not from an exaggerated side angle. His other foot, not the pivot foot, is to be positioned in front of the pitcher's rubber. He must stand so that he faces the batter. When the pitcher is in such a position and comes to a complete stop, with his gloved and bare hand holding the ball in front of him, he is in the set position.

As with the windup, the pitcher has only three options from the set position. The pitcher may step off the rubber after he achieves a set position. He may also attempt a pickoff, or he may pitch to the batter. To avoid a balk from the set position, the pitcher, when stepping off the rubber, must step back, away from home plate, with his pivot foot. Once in the set position, any action taken by the pitcher which is related to his pitching motion requires that, without hesitation or change, he continue his motion and pitch to the batter.

A pitcher may stretch before coming to the set position. That is, he may move naturally to prepare himself to come to the set position. After the stretch, however, he must come to a complete stop with the ball held in front of his body with two hands.

Before starting the stretch, the pitcher shall stand with one arm at his side. He must then proceed to the set position without hesitation and in one flowing motion. There must be a complete stop, noted by the umpires, after the stretch and before the pitcher starts to throw from the set position. When a complete stop is not made, the umpire shall promptly call a balk on the pitcher. After arriving at a complete stop, any action taken by the pitcher which is related to his pitching motion requires that, without hesitation or change, he continue his motion and pitch to the batter.

While in the set position, a pitcher must touch the rubber with the entire width of his shoe. He may not touch only the shorter side of the rubber with one edge of his shoe when pitching.

General Rules. These rules apply to both windup and set positions. Before a pitcher is required by the rules to complete his pitching motion, a pitcher may attempt to pick off a runner at any base. He must, however, step toward that base before he throws. It is a balk if the pitcher does not step at all or steps after he throws.

An illegal pitch with no runners on base shall be called a ball. If the batter attains first base by a hit or other means on that illegal pitch, he shall be permitted to advance as if the pitch were legal.

A pitcher not on the rubber who overthrows a base in an attempted pickoff is considered an infielder. As soon as the pitcher's pivot foot steps back off the rubber, the rules which apply to fielders' overthrows are in force.

When a ball drops from the pitcher's hand with no men on base it is no pitch and does not count. If, however, after the ball is dropped, it crosses either foul line, a ball shall be called. If there are men on base, a balk shall be called by the umpire.

IX. Batting

A batter must bat with both feet on or within the lines of the batter's box. He may not leave and reenter the batter's box except according to the rules. There may be no changes in the batting order except for legal substitutions. The first batter in each inning after the first inning is the batter in the order who follows the last player to complete his time at bat in the offensive team's last inning.

IN THE BATTER'S BOX
A batter may not delay his slated entry into the batter's box. When a batter will not enter the batter's

box, the umpire may then direct the pitcher to pitch. The umpire may call each pitch a strike until three strikes are called and the batter is declared out. The batter may enter the batter's box after each such strike is called, but the ball and strike count stands.

A batter may not leave the batter's box without risk unless he has requested the umpire to call time. If a batter does leave the batter's box when time has not been called and a pitch is delivered, the umpire then determines whether the pitch shall be called a ball or a strike.

After a pitcher starts his windup or comes to a set position, the batter may not leave the batter's box. When a pitch is delivered and a batter has illegally left the batter's box, the umpire determines whether the pitch shall be called a ball or a strike.

Once the windup has begun or the pitcher has come to a set position, despite the request for time by a batter, another player, or the manager, the umpire may not call time. All reasons in this circumstance, including foreign objects in eyes or on glasses or missed signs, are considered invalid.

A batter may not leave the batter's box to apply rosin or any other substance to his bat or hands unless the game has been delayed for another reason or the umpire determines that adverse weather requires such action.

Umpire's Note: Time requested by a batter in the batter's box may be called by an umpire, but the rules should be enforced so that batters are aware of their responsibility to stay in the batter's box ready to bat. This is not to be interpreted so that pitchers may unduly delay on the mound while the batter is in position in the batter's box. The umpire, in such a case, may allow a batter to leave the batter's box for a brief period of time.

When a batter illegally leaves the batter's box, thus causing a pitcher not to make a pitch, if that pitcher had already begun his windup or come to a set position, the ensuing balk is offset by the batter's infraction. Time is to be called by the umpire and the balk nullified.

When a batter becomes a runner or is put out, he has officially completed his turn at bat.

GROUND RULE DOUBLES AND HOME RUNS
The batter becomes a runner when he hits a fair fly ball over a fence that is at least 250 feet from home plate. Upon legally circling the bases, the batter is credited with a home run. If the fair fly ball is hit over a fence which is less than 250 feet from home plate, the batter is credited with a ground rule double and may advance no further than second base.

A ground rule double is awarded when a fair fly ball goes

under, through, or lodges in a fence, scoreboard, or vegetation on a fence. Runners already on base advance two bases, and the batter stops at second base. A batter is also awarded a ground rule double when his hit lands in fair ground and then, after being touched by a fielder, bounces over, under, or through a fence or into the stands, whether fair or foul. Runners already on base advance two bases and the batter stops at second base.

If a fielder touches a fair fly ball and it then bounces over a fence or into the stands in foul ground, the umpire shall call a ground rule double. But if a fair fly ball is touched by a fielder at least 250 feet from home plate and it then bounces over a fence or into the stands in fair ground, it is a home run. If touched less than 250 feet from home plate, it is a ground rule double.

BECOMING A RUNNER
When the batter hits a ball in fair ground, he is then a runner. The ball is in play, and the batter becomes a runner despite his batted ball hitting an umpire or other runner in fair ground if the ball previously had passed by any fielder except the pitcher or hit any fielder, including the pitcher.

AFTER A THIRD STRIKE
If a third called strike is not held by the catcher, the batter becomes a runner unless there is already a runner on first base or even with a runner on first base if there are also two outs. When a third strike is not held by the catcher but the batter returns to and touches any part of the dugout, the batter is out. Before the batter touches the dugout, however, he may turn around and seek to reach first base before he is tagged or thrown out.

WALKS
The batter proceeds to first base after he receives four balls (a walk, a base on balls). A substitution cannot be made for the batter who has walked until that batter touches first base. *Note:* Runners on base are not forced to advance until first base is touched by the batter. If a forced runner advances past the base to which he is entitled, he may be tagged out.

HIT BY A PITCH
A batter is awarded first base when he or his clothing is hit by a pitched ball. The batter, however, shall not be awarded first base when he does not attempt to get out of the path of or while swinging at a pitched ball or when he is hit by a ball in the strike zone. If a batter is hit by a pitch in the strike zone, it is called a strike regardless of his efforts to get out of the way. If a batter has not attempted to get out of the way and is hit by

a pitched ball out of the strike zone, it is, nevertheless, called a ball.

BATTING OUT OF ORDER
A batter who does not bat in his rightful order is declared out only when the next batter makes out or becomes a runner and an appeal is made by the opposing team. An umpire may not make any reference to a player batting out of turn unless an appeal is first made by the defensive team. Before an illegal batter has completed his turn at bat, the rightful batter may be inserted back into the correct place in the batting order and assumes the ball and strike count.

74

If an appeal is not made after the illegal batter completes his turn at bat and before the next pitch to a batter on either team, there can be no valid appeal. The game then continues, the preceding action is legal, and the batting order resumes as if the illegal batter was legal. The next player to bat is the player in the batting order following the player who batted out of turn.

If a valid appeal is made, the batter who did not bat in his rightful order is called out. The next player to bat is the player in the batting order following the player who was called out. No runs may score or runners advance as a result of the illegal batter's efforts. Advances by runners on base because of balks, passed balls, wild

pitches, or stolen bases are legal even when they occur during the time players bat out of order.

ILLEGAL BATS
If in the umpire's judgment a batter uses or prepares to use a bat which has been waxed, made flat, hollowed out, filled in, imbedded with nails, or in any manner changed to alter the flight or increase the distance of a batted ball, the batter is to be called out and removed from the game. The league president, upon review, may initiate his own disciplinary action. No runs or advances by runners when such an illegal bat is used may stand, but all outs made will count.

LEAVING THE BATTER'S BOX
A batter is out if he leaves one batter's box and enters the other after the pitcher steps on the rubber with the ball. The batter is also out if he hits a pitched ball while out of the batter's box. It does not matter if the ball is hit fair or foul or if the batter is partially or fully out of the batter's box. The batter is also out for leaving the batter's box to swing at a pitched ball during an intentional walk.

INTERFERENCE WITH THE CATCHER
The Batter Out. The umpire shall call the batter out for any action, including leaving the batter's box,

which impedes the catcher's play. When interference is called, the ball is dead and the batter is out. Runners may not advance on an interference call and must return to the bases they had last touched, in the umpire's judgment, before interference was called.

The Batter Not Out. When a batter interferes with the catcher but a runner is thrown out on the same play, the batter is not out. The runner thrown out remains out, and other runners advance at their own risk. The batter is not out if a runner trying to score is called out because of the batter's interference. In situations described in this paragraph, the rules provide that the interference call shall have no effect.

Called Strikes. A strike shall be called against a batter who swings and misses but, as he completes a circle with his bat, accidentally hits the ball with his backswing before the catcher gains possession of the ball. A strike shall also be called against a batter who, in the course of swinging at a pitch, accidentally hits the catcher with his bat.

THE BATTER PUT OUT
When a batter is tagged or first base touched by a fielder with the ball in his possession before the batter touches first base, after the batter has hit the ball fair or after a missed third strike, the batter is out. When a fielder catches the

batter's fair or foul fly ball before it touches the ground, the batter is out.

The Batter Declared Out by the Umpire. The batter shall be declared out for intentionally changing the path of a foul ball in any way after it has left his bat and he has started running to first base. The batter shall also be declared out when he is hit by his own fair ball before that ball is touched by a fielder. And when an infield fly is called by an umpire, the batter is automatically out.

Running Outside of the First Base Line. When, in the second forty-five feet of the first base line, the batter runs to the left of the foul line or to the right of the restraining line, which is itself three feet to the right of the foul line, the batter is out if, in the umpire's judgment, the batter interferes with the fielder receiving the throw to first base. The batter is required to run outside the base lines in order to avoid contact with a fielder pursuing the batted ball.

Runner Interference. The batter is called out when a runner on the bases intentionally interferes with a fielder in the midst of completing a play. The umpire shall be the sole judge of whether or not the interference was intentional.

Intentionally Dropped Balls. With less than two outs, a runner on first, or two runners on any combination of bases but second and third, or three runners on base, if a

fielder intentionally drops a line drive or a fair fly ball, the ball is dead. The batter is out, and runners return to their own bases. *Umpire's Note:* If the ball is not intentionally dropped and the infield fly rule is not called, the batter is not out and the ball is in play.

Steals of Home. The batter is out when a runner attempting to steal home, with two outs and two strikes on the batter, is hit in the strike zone by a legal pitch. The run does not score, and the inning ends. In the same situation, except that there are less than two outs, the batter is out, the ball is dead, but the run counts.

Third Strikes. If a third strike is legally caught on a fly by the catcher, the batter is out. A ball is not considered legally caught if it gets stuck in the catcher's equipment or uniform or is caught after it bounces off the umpire. The batter is out even if the catcher does not catch a third strike if there is already a runner on first base and there are less than two outs. A foul bunt on the third strike retires the batter, as does a third called or swinging strike. When a pitch is foul-tipped off the catcher's glove and is then trapped by the catcher with both hands against his chest protector or body, the batter, if it is the third strike, is out.

The Batter Hit by His Own Ball. If before a fielder touches a ball hit by the batter, the ball hits the batter in fair ground, the batter is out. The batter's box is in foul territory, so a batter hit by a batted ball in the batter's box is not out.

The Bat Hits a Batted Ball. If the batter hits or bunts a fair ball and the ball is then struck again in fair ground by the bat, the ball is dead, runners may not advance, and the batter is out. The batter is not out if, after hitting or bunting the ball, he drops his bat and the ball rolls against it. The batter shall not be out and the ball shall remain in play only if the umpire determines that the batter did not intentionally cause the bat to hit the ball a second time.

Broken Bats. There is no interference if a batted ball is struck by or strikes the broken portion of a bat in fair ground. If the broken bat and a ball collide in foul ground, the ball is foul. There is no interference if the broken portion of a bat strikes a runner or a fielder.

Bats on the Field. When a bat in one piece flies out of a batter's hands and interferes with a fielder trying to make a play in fair ground, the batter is out for interference. No distinction is made between an intentional or accidental release of the bat.

The Batting Helmet Hits a Batted Ball. The ball is considered foul if it hits a batting helmet or anything else foreign to the playing surface in foul territory. A ball which accidentally strikes a batting helmet remains in play. No distinction is made between helmets on or off the player. When a runner, in the umpire's judgment, intentionally throws his helmet at a thrown or batted ball, the runner is out, other runners are required to return to their bases, and the ball is dead.

DESIGNATED HITTER

A manager in a league that accepts the designated hitter rule may but is not required to designate a batter to hit for the starting pitcher and any relief pitchers who may enter the game. This offensive substitution does not alter any other rule concerning pitchers. The designation of such a hitter must be entered on the official lineup presented before the game to the chief umpire. Once the lineup without a designated hitter is accepted by the chief umpire, a designated hitter may not be used in that game. A designated hitter may not be used as a pinch runner.

A designated hitter may be removed for a pinch hitter, who then may remain in the lineup as the new designated hitter. The rules of substitution are applicable: a designated hitter removed from a game for any cause may not return to that game.

When the designated hitter is also inserted in the lineup as a fielder, he continues to bat in the same order as indicated on the starting lineup card. The pitcher, however, must then bat in place of the defensive player substituted for in the field by the designated hitter. A manager who makes one or more additional defensive substitutions at the same time a designated hitter is given a defensive position is allowed to decide where in the batting order the pitcher and those substitute fielders shall bat. In that case, the pitcher may be assigned a place in the batting order other than that of the fielder substituted for by the designated hitter.

When a pinch runner replaces the designated hitter on the bases, the pinch runner enters the batting order as the designated hitter. The position of designated hitter in the game lineup no longer exists when a pinch hitter, after his time at bat, enters the game as a relief pitcher; when a designated hitter takes a defensive position in the field or is pinch-hit for by the game pitcher; or when the game pitcher takes another defensive position.

Designated Hitters in Inter-League Play. A designated hitter can be used in All-Star games only if both the leagues and teams agree. A designated hitter rule is used in the World Series only in even number years—in 1982, not in 1983. In exhibition games, the rule is used if the league of the home team uses the rule during its regular season.

X. Running

A runner must touch each base in its turn: first, second, third base, and home plate. When a runner is required to return to base and the ball is dead, the runner must take the shortest return route. Thus, if required to return from third to first base, the runner should cut across the pitcher's mound. If, however, the ball is in play, a returning runner must contact all bases in the reverse direction: home plate, third, second, first base.

A runner is on base when he legally touches that base and is not out. Once legally on a base, the runner may not return to a base he came from after the pitcher, with the ball in his possession, has stepped on the rubber. A runner has a right to a base he has reached unless he is called out or forced ahead by another runner. A base may not be legally occupied by two or more runners. If two runners touch the same base at the same time while the ball is not dead, the runner ahead has the right to the base. If the trailing runner is tagged while two such runners are on one base, the trailing runner is out. The runner who had the first legal right to the base, even if tagged, is not out.

RUNNERS ADVANCE AND MAY NOT BE PUT OUT

Home Runs. The batter and all runners already on base may touch all bases in order, each runner reaching home plate, when a fair batted ball goes over the fence or into the stands. All runners and the batter may also proceed around the bases to score, without risk of being put out when, in the umpire's judgment, the direction of a fair batted ball, which would have gone over the fence or into the stands for a home run, is altered by the improper use of any part of a fielder's uniform or by any other object, including his glove, thrown by him.

Runners Advance Three Bases. When a fielder intentionally touches a fair *batted* ball by throwing his glove or making improper use of any part of his uniform, such as his hat or mask, the umpire shall award three bases to the batter and runners. The ball remains in play. The batter may attempt to reach home plate but may be put out once he goes beyond third base.

Runners Advance Two Bases. When a fair ball bounces off the ground or a player and then into the stands alongside the first or third base lines or under or through a fence, scoreboard, or vegetation on a fence, the umpire shall award two bases to the batter and runners.

When a fielder intentionally *throws* his glove or other object or intentionally and improperly uses any part of his uniform, such as his hat or mask, to touch a thrown ball, the umpire shall award two bases to the batter and runners.

When a ball is thrown over, under, into, or through a fence or into or onto the screen atop the backstop or other protective spectator screens, the umpire shall award two bases to the batter and runners.

Umpire's Note: The award of bases to runners by the umpire shall be determined by the position of the runners when the errant throw was made. When the errant throw is the first play by an infielder, however, then the position of the runners when the ball was pitched shall guide the umpire. In circumstances requiring the award of two bases, the ball is dead.

Runners Advance One Base. When a pitcher commits a balk, the umpire shall award all runners one base, excluding the batter. When the batter is awarded first base, as when he is walked or hit by a pitch, a runner forced shall also be awarded one base.

When the pitcher on the rubber attempts to pick off a runner or pitches to a batter and the ball goes into the stands or dugout or over, under, in, or through a fence or screen, the ball is dead and runners shall be awarded one base.

When the batter reaches first base because of a walk or as the result of a third strike not caught by the catcher and the last pitch— the fourth ball or third strike—

passes the catcher and sticks in the umpire's equipment, the batter is advanced to second base.

When the batter is interfered with by the catcher or any other defensive player, a runner making an effort to steal on the same play shall be awarded one base.

When the runners advance one base as a result of a wild pitch, which is also the fourth ball or third strike, the batter is, nevertheless, awarded only first base.

Runners may go past the bases to which they are directed by the umpire but at their own risk. If a runner who has gone past a base is tagged for the inning-ending third out before a runner ahead of him who has been forced home has scored, the run, nevertheless, counts.

A Fielder Falls into the Stands. If after making a legal catch, the fielder falls into the stands or into the dugout or falls down while in the dugout, the ball is dead and each runner on base shall be awarded one base by the umpire. If the fielder, after catching the ball in the dugout, does not fall down, the batter is out, the ball is in play, and runners may advance only at their own risk.

Obstruction of the Runner. It is the umpire's responsibility to indicate, by voice or sign (both arms held in the air), when a fielder has obstructed a runner. Such obstruction shall be called when a fielder without control of the ball hinders the movement of a runner toward a base. At the time obstruction is called, the ball is dead. The effect of a call of obstruction on a batter going to first base or on another runner on whom a play is being made is that all runners shall be awarded by the umpire those bases they would have reached if the obstruction had not occurred. In every case, the runner who was obstructed shall be allowed to proceed a minimum of one base from the base he last legally occupied. All runners forced by the award of an additional base to an obstructed runner may advance without risk.

Umpire's Note: Obstruction is not called immediately if a play on the obstructed runner is not in process. Such a runner may advance on his own. When the umpire judges that the play is over, he calls time and rectifies any inequities caused by the obstruction of the runner. When circumstances warrant that the call of obstruction be delayed, a runner who passes the base he would have been entitled to by the call of obstruction proceeds at his own risk.

Wild Throws before Obstruction Is Called. If a ball has left the hand of a fielder in the process of throwing, a following call of obstruction shall not prevent the umpire from allowing runners to advance because of an ensuing errant throw. For example, when a runner headed toward third base is obstructed by a fielder as a thrown ball goes into the stands in back of third base, the runner shall be entitled to score and all other runners shall be awarded two bases in addition to the bases they occupied before the call of obstruction.

Obstruction at Home Plate. A catcher without control of the ball may not stand in the way of or interfere with a runner trying to score. If any fielder, including the catcher, without control of the ball, blocks home plate or makes contact with the batter or his bat when a runner is attempting to steal home or score on a squeeze play, the ball shall be declared dead. The runner shall be awarded home plate, and the batter shall be awarded first base. The pitcher shall be charged with a balk because of the catcher's actions.

INTERFERENCE BY OFFENSIVE PLAYERS (I)
The umpire, when interference is called, shall also call the ball dead and the runner out, except when these rules specifically contradict that principle.

Interference by Batters. With a runner on third base and less than two outs, if the batter impedes any fielder trying to make a play at home plate, the runner shall be called out.

When the batter hits or bunts a fair ball and the ball is then struck again in fair ground by the bat,

82

83

the ball is dead, runners may not advance, and the batter is out. The batter is not out if, after hitting or bunting the ball, he drops his bat and the ball rolls against it. The batter shall not be out and the ball shall remain in play only if the umpire determines that the batter did not intentionally cause the bat to hit the ball a second time.

When, in the second forty-five feet of the first base line, the batter runs to the left of the foul line or to the right of the restraining line, which is itself three feet to the right of the foul line, the batter is out if, in the umpire's judgment, the batter interferes with the fielder trying to field the ball or receiving the throw to first base. Running within that restraining lane shall be defined as running with both feet within or on the lines which mark that lane. The batter, however, is required to run outside the base line or restraining lane in order to avoid contact with a fielder pursuing a batted ball.

The batter is out if he intentionally interferes with any fielder playing a batted ball or interferes, intentionally or not, with a catcher's effort to field the ball after the third strike. The batter is also out if he intentionally changes the course of a foul ball by any means.

Interference by Runners. A runner who intentionally alters the course of a thrown ball shall be called out for interference. And a runner who cannot evade a collision with a fielder playing a batted ball shall also be called out for interference. When a runner collides with a fielder or fielders and more than one fielder is making an effort to play a batted ball, the runner shall be called out only if he collided, in the umpire's judgment, with the fielder with the right to the ball.

When a batted ball in fair ground passes by an infielder and hits a runner right behind that infielder, the ball is in play and the runner is not out. *Umpire's Note*: In this circumstance, the runner is out for being hit with a batted ball if the ball was playable by another infielder. A runner shall, nevertheless, be called out if, after the ball passes by the infielder, the ball is intentionally kicked by the runner.

INTERFERENCE BY OFFENSIVE PLAYERS (II)

Double Plays. A base runner who interferes with a batted ball or a fielder playing a batted ball is out. If that interference is intentional and its open purpose, in the umpire's judgment, is to break up a double play, then no runners may advance, nor may they score because of the interference, and the batter shall be called out.

If a batter openly seeks to break up a double play by intentional interference with a batted ball or a fielder playing a batted ball, the runner who is closest to scoring, as well as the batter, shall be called out, and in no case shall any runner advance because of the interference.

After an Out. A runner or batter who has been put out and then interferes with the continuation of play as it affects another runner shall cause that other runner to be called out. A batter or runner shall not be called out for interference merely for continuing to run on the base paths after he has been put out unless, in the umpire's judgment, that runner has actually disconcerted or interfered with the defensive team.

INTERFERENCE BY COACHES AND OTHERS

A runner shall be called out when, in the umpire's judgment, the runner has been physically aided by a coach. A runner on third base shall be called out if the third base coach, not within the coach's box, attempts to cause a fielder to throw to third base.

An umpire shall call out a runner attempting to reach a base near which there are one or more members of his team who, in any manner, physical or not, are trying to interfere with the defensive team's effort to put out that runner.

Interference shall be called when any member of the offensive team fails to leave the dugout, coach's box, on-deck circle, or any other area of which the space is needed for a fielder making a play on a batted or thrown ball. The target of the fielder's play, batter or runner, shall be called out.

APPEAL PLAYS

To be valid, appeals must be initiated by the defensive team after the infraction and before the next pitch, play, or attempted play. If the infraction is followed immediately by a third out, the appeal must be initiated before all defensive infielders and the pitcher have crossed the foul lines going toward the bench.

Once a specific appeal is made, it may not be reinitiated if unsuccessful. Two consecutive appeals are unacceptable on one runner for the same infraction at the same base on the same play. Thus, in the process of making an appeal, if a ball thrown to a base goes into the dugout, the ball is dead and another appeal is barred. An appeal is in no manner to be thought of as a play or an attempted play.

An appeal is not valid if it is not presented by actions or words that leave no doubt in the umpire's mind as to the intention of the defensive team. Thus, a fielder who steps on third base with the ball in his possession on his way to the dugout to repair his glove would not satisfy this appeal rule.

If on the same play that retires the batting team, an out by appeal and an out under other conditions is made, the out by appeal takes precedence. For example, with one out a runner tags up and leaves third base too early on a fly ball to the outfield, which is caught for the second out. Meanwhile, the runner from second base, who has legally tagged up, is thrown out running for third base but only after the runner from third base had crossed home plate. On appeal, the runner who left third base too early is called out, and because the appeal takes precedence, the run does not score.

If an umpire on a play which retires the batting team calls two or more outs on two or more different appeals, the defensive team may choose the out or outs that most improve its tactical situation.

Runners Out on Appeal. A runner who is out on appeal for failing to touch or retouch a base does not change in any manner the position or standing of a runner behind him on the bases. If, however, there are two outs and a runner is then called out on appeal, no runners behind him may be allowed to score.

No runners behind or before the runner called for the third out on appeal may be allowed to score if a force play is the source of that third out.

When a runner does not touch home plate and a following runner does, no matter how close in time the actions occurred, if the first runner is called out on appeal or is

tagged out for the third out before he touches the plate, the following runner's score is disallowed. The run does not count, even though the following runner touched home plate before the third out was recorded.

After a runner slides or runs past first base and does not directly return to that base, the runner is out if he or the base is tagged before he retouches it.

When a runner misses home plate and makes no effort to go back to that base, he is out when home plate is tagged.

A runner is out if, after a batted ball is caught in the air and before he can return to his last legally occupied base, he or the base is tagged.

A runner is out if he tags up by taking a running start from behind the base.

Missed Bases. When the ball is in play, runners are required to touch all bases in order, whether advancing or returning to a base. When a runner misses a base, he is out if he or that base is tagged before he returns to it.

When a runner misses a base, he cannot return to it if a runner following him has scored. A runner also cannot return to a missed base after he has touched the next base and the ball has been called dead.

WHEN RUNNERS ARE OUT
Tag-Outs. Runners are out if, with

the ball not dead, they are tagged when not legally occupying a base. A runner is not out, however, if he is tagged after he arrives safely at a base that is dislodged by the impact of the runner. A trailing runner shall be considered to have made contact with the dislodged base if, in the opinion of the umpire, the trailing runner made contact with the space formerly occupied by the dislodged base.

Force Plays. A runner who has been forced is out when he or the base he is attempting to reach is tagged. If, however, the runner behind him is put out, there is no more force and the runner is not out unless tagged. If a runner touches and then goes past the base to which he is forced, he also is not out unless tagged. If a forced runner, after reaching the base to which he is forced, reverses himself and proceeds back toward the base he came from, he is again in a force play situation. If the runner reverses himself to intentionally confuse the fielders or make a travesty of the game, he shall be called out.

Runners Hit by a Batted Ball. If, before a fair batted ball passes by or is touched by a fielder, the ball hits a runner in fair ground, the runner is out and the ball is dead. Runners, other than those runners who are forced on the play, are not allowed to move ahead on the bases.

Infield Flies. When an infield fly is

called and the batted ball strikes a runner who is, at the same time, touching a base, the runner is not out. When that runner is not touching a base and is hit by an infield fly, he is out. In both cases, under this rule the batter is out.

At Home Plate. When the batter interferes with a play at home plate, the runner trying to score is called out. If, however, in the same situation, there are two outs, the batter is called out. In both cases, under this rule the run does not score.

Passing a Runner. A runner is called out for running past another runner on the bases, unless the runner ahead has been already put out.

Missing Home Plate. When the runner does not continue toward his dugout after missing home plate but quickly tries to return to that base, he must be tagged to be put out. If a runner misses home plate and makes no effort to return to that base, however, he is out when an appeal is made and home plate is tagged. The purpose of this rule is to assure that a catcher is not obligated to pursue a runner who, after missing home plate, heads back toward the dugout.

Travesty of the Game. A runner, once having legally acquired a base, may not run the bases in reverse order to intentionally confuse fielders or make a travesty of the game. The umpire shall call time as soon as the infraction occurs, and the runner shall be called out. If, however, a runner legally advances to a base and then, by his own misunderstanding or the actions of fielders, is convinced to return to his previous base, he may be put out. If he reaches and makes contact with his previously held base, he is safe and may not be tagged out.

At First Base. A batter running to first base who runs or slides past the base and does not directly return to the base, is out. When that runner, instead of directly returning to the base, heads for second base and is tagged, he is out. When that runner, instead of directly returning to the base, heads for his fielding position or the dugout and he or first base is tagged, he is out on appeal.

A run counts if scored before a runner who did not directly return to first base is called out if that runner had originally touched first base.

After a Fly Ball. After a fly ball, fair or foul, is legally caught, the runner is out on appeal if, before he can retouch his base, he or his base is tagged. The appeal must be made in a timely manner, that is, before the next pitch or play.

Foul Tips. A foul tip is not considered a fly ball. The runner must return to base if a foul tip is not caught. When the foul tip is caught by the catcher, however, the runner may proceed on the bases as if the foul tip were a swinging missed strike.

Interference. A runner who inten-tionally alters the course of a thrown ball shall be called out for interference. And a runner who impedes a fielder playing a batted ball shall also be called out for interference.

Interference with a fielder by a runner need not be intentional to cause the runner to be called out except when that runner, either in fair or foul ground, is legally on a base when the interference occurs. When a runner legally on a base does not intentionally interfere with a fielder, then that runner may not be called out even if he does in some manner impede a fielder.

If interference by a runner is called with less than two outs, both the runner and the batter are called out. Only the batter is called out if there are two outs when the interference is called.

Interference in a Rundown. When a runner in a rundown interferes with a fielder, a following runner who has reached and occupies the base immediately behind the runner called out for interference shall be directed by the umpire to return to his previously held base.

Leaving the Base Line. When seeking to evade a tag, a runner, unless trying to avoid hindering a fielder making a play on a batted ball, shall be called out for running more than three feet outside the base line. The base line is defined as a straight line between bases.

A runner who crosses first base

and then leaves the base line, not openly appearing to be trying to advance to the next base, shall be called out. A runner is out when he crosses first base and then leaves the base line to proceed toward his defensive position or dugout if the umpire believes the runner has given up any further attempt to run the bases. Other runners may advance, and the ball is in play.

A batter who misses a third strike that is not caught by the catcher is not out until he enters the dugout. If the runner stops before he enters the dugout, he may attempt to reach first base and will be safe unless tagged or thrown out.

XI. Substituting Players

Anytime during the game when the ball is dead, a manager may substitute a player or players.

When a player has been replaced, that player shall leave the playing field, and he shall not be allowed to take further part in the game.* The substitute player shall bat in the replaced player's position in the batting order.

If the manager of the defensive team sends in more than one substitute at the same time, he must tell the umpire-in-chief immediately what positions the new fielders shall take in the batting order.

*If a substitute takes the place of a player-manager, the player-manager may, if he so chooses, continue to manage from one of the coaching lines.

If the umpire is not informed immediately about the batting order, he shall decide in what order the substitutes shall bat.

XII. Disrupting Play

Urging demonstrations by spectators or using words which ridicule the opposition, umpires, or fans by anyone officially connected with either team is prohibited. There may be no physical contact with an umpire.

While the ball is in play, no member of a team may call time or use any other means to trick the pitcher into balking.

The batter may not be distracted by a fielder who stations himself in the batter's field of vision and acts in an unsportsmanlike manner.

EJECTION

Immediately upon ejection a participant must leave the playing field. He may have nothing further to do with the game. He may not return to the team bench. If he goes into the stands, he must not be in a team uniform and must not remain anywhere near his bench or bull pen.

A person suspended may not enter the bench area, bull pen, or press box during a game.

Disorderly protests from the bench are prohibited. The umpire will first notify the bench to stop disorderly protest. If the protest persists, the umpire may direct the disorderly person to his clubhouse. If the umpire cannot identify those who are causing the disturbance, then he may order all persons on the bench into their clubhouse. The manager, however, may recall any player when needed for entry into the game as a substitute.

XIII. Suspending Play

Once a baseball game has begun, the umpire-in-chief shall try to do everything in his power to see that the game is completed. An umpire should suspend or terminate a game only when no possibility of playing the game remains.

Once play has been suspended because of inclement weather or because of the poor condition of the playing field, the umpire-in-chief shall not call for resumption of play until at least thirty minutes have elapsed. Suspension of play, however, may continue for as long as necessary.

When there is a delay in the game or a suspension of play, the umpire-in-chief has jurisdiction over the groundskeeper and his crew. The umpire-in-chief is the final authority in deciding whether or not the field has been rendered fit for play. If the groundskeeper does not cooperate with the umpire-in-chief in this matter, the umpire may forfeit the game, declaring the visiting team the winner.

When a game is called by the umpire because of playing field machinery failure, legal curfew, time limit, or darkness, the game is to be completed from the point of suspension at a future date. Only those reasons specifically cited in the rules may be used to justify a suspended game.

If a game is called by the umpire because of adverse weather after five full innings have been played but before an inning in progress has been completed, it is called a suspended game when in that inning the visiting team has tied the score and the home team is scoreless or the visiting team has taken the lead and the home team has not tied the game or again taken the lead. If the game is tied and the above special circumstances concerning suspension during incomplete innings do not apply, the entire game must be played again.

To be suspended, at least five full innings of a game must have been completed before the suspension. A game, however, terminated because of darkness or the failure of playing field machinery (for example, water removal machinery) need not be a regulation game and stands suspended whenever such a decision is made by the umpire.

Weather is the first consideration when determining whether a game called by the umpire can be deemed suspended.

90

RULES FOR COMPLETING A SUSPENDED GAME

A suspended game is to be completed as soon as the rules allow. When the game is continued, the batting orders and fielders' positions shall be exactly as they were when the game was suspended. Substitutions are allowed according to the rules: players substituted for in the suspended portion of the game may not play in the continued portion of the game; and players available as substitutes in the suspended portion of the game are eligible to play in the continued portion of the game.

A player joining the team after the game in question was suspended may not substitute despite his acquisition as a replacement for a player no longer with the team if that player had been removed from the game before the suspension.

If a pitcher who was announced as a reliever just before the suspension of play does not get the third out or pitch to a batter who subsequently reaches first base and that pitcher does not start the continued portion of the suspended game, he may not return to the game.

SCHEDULING A SUSPENDED GAME

A suspended game is to be completed before the next regularly scheduled single game on the same field between the two teams. If no single game between the two

teams remains, then the continued game is to be played before the next regularly scheduled doubleheader.

When there are no more playing dates on the same field, then the suspended game is to be continued before the first single game—or if there are no more single games left on the schedule, then before the first scheduled doubleheader—on the home field of the visiting team. If there are no open dates left between the two teams, then the game is permanently called and will not be continued.

DOUBLEHEADERS

A maximum of two championship official games can be played on one date. Suspended game continuations do not count toward the two-game maximum. It is the first game which is considered that date's regularly scheduled game. A *doubleheader* is defined as *two games played for one admission on one date*. The first game started in a doubleheader must end before the start of the second game.

There is a twenty-minute period between games of a doubleheader. The chief umpire may order an additional thirty-minute period between games if he informs both managers after the last out of the first game. Time between games is kept by the chief umpire of the first game.

The home club may petition the

league president to extend the period of time between games of a doubleheader in order to hold a special event. Approval, if granted, must be transmitted by the chief umpire at the end of the first game to both team managers.

XIV. Ending the Game

GAME LENGTH

A regulation baseball game is nine full innings. It may continue into extra innings if tied at the end of nine innings. The game ends at the end of eight and one-half innings if the home team is ahead at that point. The game ends as soon as the home team scores the winning run in its half of the ninth inning. The game may also be terminated by the umpire because of adverse weather or playing conditions.

An extra inning game ends when the home team has scored one more run than the visiting team or when, at the end of a full extra inning, the visiting team has scored one more run than the home team.

A game which is ended by the umpire after five full innings are played is a regulation game. It is also a regulation game if ended after the home team scores to tie the game in the bottom half of the fifth inning. A tie is any regulation game which ends with both teams having scored the same number of runs. If a game ends before it is a regulation game, it is not counted—it is no game. The home team wins if the game ends after the first half of the fifth inning and at the point the home team has scored more runs than the visiting team.

FINAL SCORE

The final score is the number of runs tallied by each team at the game's end. A regulation game ends either at the end of eight and one-half innings if the home team is ahead at that time or after nine full innings if the visiting team is ahead at that time. Games end as soon as the winning run is scored. If the home team scores the winning run in the last half of the ninth inning or extra inning, the game ends when the winning run crosses the home plate. If, however, a game ends with a home run over the fence, all runners on base are allowed to score and the game ends when the batter circles the bases and touches home plate. If the batter who has hit the home run or a runner previously on base passes a runner ahead of him, the game ends as soon as the winning run crosses home plate.

CALLED GAME

If a game is called, it ends when that decision is announced by the umpire. If, however, a game is called before an inning in progress is completed, the score reverts to that of the last completed full inning when in that incomplete inning the visiting team tied the score and the home team is scoreless or the visiting team has taken the lead and the home team has not tied the game or again taken the lead.

FORFEITS

A forfeit may be granted to the opposition under the following circumstances:

1) when a team at the beginning of a game is not ready or willing to play within five minutes after the chief umpire has announced play if in the opinion of the chief umpire that failure is avoidable;
2) when a team is not ready or willing to start the second game of a doubleheader on time;
3) when a team obviously tries to extend, shorten, or delay a game;
4) when a team does not continue play, unless the umpire has called or suspended the game;
5) when a team will not continue within one minute after an umpire calls play during the course of a game;
6) when a team, after previous warning, consciously and continually breaks the rules;
7) when a player does not, within a reasonable length of time, obey an umpire when ordered to leave the game;
8) when a team cannot or will not field nine players; and
9) when, after a game has been suspended, the home team, that is, its groundskeepers, will not ready the field for play as directed to by the umpire.

An umpire is to foward a written report of a forfeit to the league president within twenty-four hours, but failure to do so does not invalidate the forfeit.

93

PROTESTS

No protest can be accepted that is based on an umpire's judgment call. Protests on an umpire's alleged errors as they concern the rules are decided solely by the league president according to procedures formulated by the league. The decision of the league president is final.

Protests to be valid must be made to the umpire at the time of the play in question and before the next pitch or before a runner is put out. A game-ending play that leads to a protest allows the protest to be made with the league office until twelve P.M. the next day.

TESTING THE RULES

1) There is a runner on first base. The batter hits a sharp grounder that hits the runner before any infielder touches it. Is the batter or the runner or neither out?

2) With runners at first and second, the batter slugs a hard grounder into the outfield. The left fielder rushes forward to stop the ball, but the ball is deflected off his glove and bounces into the stands. What is the ruling?

3) With a runner on third base, there is only one out. The batter drives a long, towering fly ball toward right field, but the ball is in foul territory. To prevent the runner from tagging up and trying to score, the outfielder deliberately allows the ball to drop into foul territory. Has the outfielder violated any rule?

4) A batter has two strikes against him. The pitcher throws a fast ball that tails inside. The batter swings at the pitch and misses. The ball hits him. Does the batter take his base or is he out?

5) There is a runner on third base. There are two outs, and there are two strikes on the batter. As the pitcher goes into his windup, the runner starts for home. The pitcher throws a perfect strike, but the ball hits the runner as the runner steps on home plate. Does the run count or is the batter out?

Quick Quiz (or, Were You Really Paying Attention?)

1) A batter slugs a long hard one. The ball is sailing out of the park, and it looks like a sure home run. The ball hits the foul pole and bounces into the stands. Is the batter entitled to a home run or not?

2) A leading home run hitter comes to bat with a bat that measures forty-three inches long. Does it make any difference?

3) A runner slides into third base. He slides so hard that he actually forces the bag out of the ground. He scrambles around to touch the base again, but the third baseman tags him out. Is the runner out?

4) There is a runner at first base. The pitcher attempts to pick the runner off, but he throws the ball into the stands. How many bases may the runner advance?

5) The batter is at the plate. The pitcher tosses a fastball. The batter swings and fouls the ball back into the catcher's mask. The ball bounces off the mask of the catcher and is caught by the catcher. Is the batter out?

6) A runner is on second base. He runs back and steals first. Is this a legal steal?

Answers to Testing the Rules

1) The runner deflected the batted ball. Therefore, he is ruled out. The ball is ruled dead. The batter goes to first base.
2) If a bouncing ball is deflected by a fielder so that the ball bounces into the stands, the batter and all runners are awarded two bases. Hence, the runner on second would score. It is interesting to note, however, that until 1931, a fair ball that bounced into the stands was considered a home run!
3) No. There is no rule to prevent a fielder from allowing a foul ball to drop to the ground.
4) The batter is out.
5) The batter is out on three strikes. And the run does not count. If there had been less than two outs, the run would have counted.

Answers to Quick Quiz

1) The batter is entitled to the home run. Any ball that hits the foul pole in the outfield stands is fair.
2) It makes a difference. The player will not be allowed to bat unless he changes to a shorter bat. No bat can exceed forty-two inches in length.
3) The runner is safe. If the slide loosens the bag, no play can be made on the runner.
4) If the pitcher throws the ball into the stands, the runner may advance only one base.
5) The batter is not out. It is not a legal catch.
6) No. Stealing the bases in reverse order is not legal, and the player may be called out for making a travesty of the game.